**GENERAL APTITUDE
AND ABILITIES SERIES**

THIS IS YOUR **PASSBOOK®** FOR ...

READING COMPREHENSION

NATIONAL LEARNING CORPORATION®
passbooks.com

COPYRIGHT NOTICE

PASSBOOK® SERIES

THE *PASSBOOK® SERIES* has been created to prepare applicants and candidates for the ultimate academic battlefield – the examination room.

At some time in our lives, each and every one of us may be required to take an examination – for validation, matriculation, admission, qualification, registration, certification, or licensure.

Based on the assumption that every applicant or candidate has met the basic formal educational standards, has taken the required number of courses, and read the necessary texts, the *PASSBOOK® SERIES* furnishes the one special preparation which may assure passing with confidence, instead of failing with insecurity. Examination questions – together with answers – are furnished as the basic vehicle for study so that the mysteries of the examination and its compounding difficulties may be eliminated or diminished by a sure method.

This book is meant to help you pass your examination provided that you qualify and are serious in your objective.

The entire field is reviewed through the huge store of content information which is succinctly presented through a provocative and challenging approach – the question-and-answer method.

A climate of success is established by furnishing the correct answers at the end of each test.

You soon learn to recognize types of questions, forms of questions, and patterns of questioning. You may even begin to anticipate expected outcomes.

You perceive that many questions are repeated or adapted so that you can gain acute insights, which may enable you to score many sure points.

You learn how to confront new questions, or types of questions, and to attack them confidently and work out the correct answers.

You note objectives and emphases, and recognize pitfalls and dangers, so that you may make positive educational adjustments.

Moreover, you are kept fully informed in relation to new concepts, methods, practices, and directions in the field.

You discover that you arre actually taking the examination all the time: you are preparing for the examination by "taking" an examination, not by reading extraneous and/or supererogatory textbooks.

In short, this PASSBOOK®, used directedly, should be an important factor in helping you to pass your test.

READING COMPREHENSION
UNDERSTANDING AND INTERPRETING WRITTEN MATERIAL

COMMENTARY

The ability to read and understand written materials – texts, publications, newspapers, orders, directions, expositions – is a skill basic to a functioning democracy and to an efficient business or viable government.

That is why almost all examinations – for beginning, middle, and senior levels – test reading comprehension, directly or indirectly.

The reading test measures how well you understand what you read. This is how it is done: You read a short paragraph and five statements. From the five statements, you choose the one statement, or answer, that is BEST supported by, or best matches, what is said in the paragraph.

SAMPLE QUESTIONS

DIRECTIONS: Each question has five suggested answers, lettered A, B, C, D, and E. Decide which one is the BEST answer. *PRINT THE LETTER OF THE CORRECT ANSWER IN THE SPACE AT THE RIGHT.*

1.   The prevention of accidents makes it necessary not only that safety devices be used to guard exposed machinery but also that mechanics be instructed in safety rules which they must follow for their own protection and that the light in the plant be adequate. The paragraph BEST supports the statement that industrial accidents   1._____

   A.   are always avoidable
   B.   may be due to ignorance
   C.   usually result from inadequate machinery
   D.   cannot be entirely overcome
   E.   result in damage to machinery

ANALYSIS

Remember what you have to do–
   First   - Read the paragraph.
   Second   - Decide what the paragraph means.
   Third   - Read the five suggested answers.
   Fourth   - Select the one answer which BEST matches what the paragraph says or is BEST supported by something in the paragraph. (Sometimes you may have to read the paragraph again in order to be sure which suggested answer is best.)
This paragraph is talking about three steps that should be taken to prevent industrial accidents–

   1.   use safety devices on machines
   2.   instruct mechanics in safety rules
   3.   provide adequate lighting.

SELECTION

With this in mind let's look at each suggested answer. Each one starts with "Industrial accidents..."

SUGGESTED ANSWER A.
Industrial accidents (A) are always avoidable.
(The paragraph talks about how to avoid accidents, but does not say that accidents are always avoidable.)

SUGGESTED ANSWER B.
Industrial accidents (b) may be due to ignorance.
(One of the steps given in the paragraph to prevent accidents is to instruct mechanics on safety rules. This suggests that lack of knowledge or ignorance of safety rules causes accidents. This suggested answer sounds like a good possibility for being the right answer.)

SUGGESTED ANSWER C.
Industrial accidents (C) usually result from inadequate machinery.
(The paragraph does suggest that exposed machines cause accidents, but it doesn't say that it is the usual cause of accidents. The word usually makes this a wrong answer.)

SUGGESTED ANSWER D.
Industrial accidents (D) cannot be entirely overcome.
(You may know from your own experience that this is a true statement. But that is not what the paragraph is talking about. Therefore it is NOT the correct answer.)

SUGGESTED ANSWER E.
Industrial accidents (E) result in damage to machinery.
(This is a statement that may or may not be true, but in any case it is NOT covered by the paragraph.)

———————

Looking back, you see that the one suggested answer of the five given that BEST matches what the paragraph says is—

Industrial accidents (B) may be due to ignorance.

The CORRECT answer then is B.

Be sure you read ALL the possible answers before you make your choice. You may think that none of the five answers is really good, but choose the BEST one of the five.

———————

2. Probably few people realize, as they drive on a concrete road, that steel is used to keep   2.____
the surface flat in spite of the weight of the busses and trucks. Steel bars, deeply embedded in the concrete, provide sinews to take the stresses so that the stresses cannot
crack the slab or make it wavy.
The paragraph BEST supports the statement that a concrete road

    A.   is expensive to build
    B.   usually cracks under heavy weights
    C.   looks like any other road
    D.   is used only for heavy traffic
    E.   is reinforced with other material

ANALYSIS

This paragraph is commenting on the fact that—
    1.   few people realize, as they drive on a concrete road, that steel is deeply
embedded
    2.   steel keeps the surface flat
    3.   steel bars enable the road to take the stresses without cracking or becom-
ing wavy.

SELECTION

Now read and think about the possible answers:
    A.   A concrete road is expensive to build. (Maybe so but that is not what the paragraph
is about.)
    B.   A concrete road usually cracks under heavy weights. (The paragraph talks about
using steel bars to prevent heavy weights from cracking concrete roads. It says
nothing about how usual it is for the roads to crack. The word usually makes this
suggested answer wrong.)
    C.   A concrete road looks like any other road. (This may or may not be true. The impor-
tant thing to note is that it has nothing to do with what the paragraph is about.)
    D.   A concrete road is used only for heavy traffic. (This answer at least has something
to do with the paragraph-concrete roads are used with heavy traffic but it does not
say "used only.")
    E.   A concrete road is reinforced with other material. (This choice seems to be the cor-
rect one on two counts: First, the paragraph does suggest that concrete roads are
made stronger by embedding steel bars in them. This is another way of saying
"concrete roads are reinforced with steel bars." Second, by the process of elimination, the other four choices are ruled out as correct answers simply because they
do not apply.)

You can be sure that not all the reading questions will be so easy as these.

_____

HINTS FOR ANSWERING READING QUESTIONS

1. Read the paragraph carefully. Then read each suggested answer carefully. Read every word, because often one word can make the difference between a right and a wrong answer.

2. Choose that answer which is supported in the paragraph itself. Do not choose an answer which is a correct statement unless it is based on information in the paragraph.

3. Even though a suggested answer has many of the words used in the paragraph, it may still be wrong.

4. Look out for words – such as *always, never, entirely, or only* – which tend to make a suggested answer wrong.

5. Answer first those questions which you can answer most easily. Then work on the other questions.

6. If you can't figure out the answer to the question, guess.

HOW TO TAKE A TEST

You have studied long, hard and conscientiously.

With your official admission card in hand, and your heart pounding, you have been admitted to the examination room.

You note that there are several hundred other applicants in the examination room waiting to take the same test.

They all appear to be equally well prepared.

You know that nothing but your best effort will suffice. The "moment of truth" is at hand: you now have to demonstrate objectively, in writing, your knowledge of content and your understanding of subject matter.

You are fighting the most important battle of your life—to pass and/or score high on an examination which will determine your career and provide the economic basis for your livelihood.

What extra, special things should you know and should you do in taking the examination?

I. YOU MUST PASS AN EXAMINATION

A. *WHAT EVERY CANDIDATE SHOULD KNOW*
Examination applicants often ask us for help in preparing for the written test. What can I study in advance? What kinds of questions will be asked? How will the test be given? How will the papers be graded?

B. *HOW ARE EXAMS DEVELOPED?*
Examinations are carefully written by trained technicians who are specialists in the field known as "psychological measurement," in consultation with recognized authorities in the field of work that the test will cover. These experts recommend the subject matter areas or skills to be tested; only those knowledges or skills important to your success on the job are included. The most reliable books and source materials available are used as references. Together, the experts and technicians judge the difficulty level of the questions.

Test technicians know how to phrase questions so that the problem is clearly stated. Their ethics do not permit "trick" or "catch" questions. Questions may have been tried out on sample groups, or subjected to statistical analysis, to determine their usefulness.

Written tests are often used in combination with performance tests, ratings of training and experience, and oral interviews. All of these measures combine to form the best-known means of finding the right person for the right job.

II. HOW TO PASS THE WRITTEN TEST

A. BASIC STEPS

1) Study the announcement

How, then, can you know what subjects to study? Our best answer is: "Learn as much as possible about the class of positions for which you've applied." The exam will test the knowledge, skills and abilities needed to do the work.

Your most valuable source of information about the position you want is the official exam announcement. This announcement lists the training and experience qualifications. Check these standards and apply only if you come reasonably close to meeting them. Many jurisdictions preview the written test in the exam announcement by including a section called "Knowledge and Abilities Required," "Scope of the Examination," or some similar heading. Here you will find out specifically what fields will be tested.

2) Choose appropriate study materials

If the position for which you are applying is technical or advanced, you will read more advanced, specialized material. If you are already familiar with the basic principles of your field, elementary textbooks would waste your time. Concentrate on advanced textbooks and technical periodicals. Think through the concepts and review difficult problems in your field.

These are all general sources. You can get more ideas on your own initiative, following these leads. For example, training manuals and publications of the government agency which employs workers in your field can be useful, particularly for technical and professional positions. A letter or visit to the government department involved may result in more specific study suggestions, and certainly will provide you with a more definite idea of the exact nature of the position you are seeking.

3) Study this book!

III. KINDS OF TESTS

Tests are used for purposes other than measuring knowledge and ability to perform specified duties. For some positions, it is equally important to test ability to make adjustments to new situations or to profit from training. In others, basic mental abilities not dependent on information are essential. Questions which test these things may not appear as pertinent to the duties of the position as those which test for knowledge and information. Yet they are often highly important parts of a fair examination. For very general questions, it is almost impossible to help you direct your study efforts. What we can do is to point out some of the more common of these general abilities needed in public service positions and describe some typical questions.

1) General information

Broad, general information has been found useful for predicting job success in some kinds of work. This is tested in a variety of ways, from vocabulary lists to questions about current events. Basic background in some field of work, such as sociology or economics, may be sampled in a group of questions. Often these are principles which have become familiar to most persons through exposure rather than through formal training. It is difficult to advise you how to study for these questions; being alert to the world around you is our best suggestion.

2) Verbal ability

An example of an ability needed in many positions is verbal or language ability. Verbal ability is, in brief, the ability to use and understand words. Vocabulary and grammar tests are typical measures of this ability. Reading comprehension or paragraph interpretation questions are common in many kinds of civil service tests. You are given a paragraph of written material and asked to find its central meaning.

IV. KINDS OF QUESTIONS

1. Multiple-choice Questions

Most popular of the short-answer questions is the "multiple choice" or "best answer" question. It can be used, for example, to test for factual knowledge, ability to solve problems or judgment in meeting situations found at work.

A multiple-choice question is normally one of three types:
- It can begin with an incomplete statement followed by several possible endings. You are to find the one ending which *best* completes the statement, although some of the others may not be entirely wrong.
- It can also be a complete statement in the form of a question which is answered by choosing one of the statements listed.
- It can be in the form of a problem – again you select the best answer.

Here is an example of a multiple-choice question with a discussion which should give you some clues as to the method for choosing the right answer:

When an employee has a complaint about his assignment, the action which will *best* help him overcome his difficulty is to
   A. discuss his difficulty with his coworkers
   B. take the problem to the head of the organization
   C. take the problem to the person who gave him the assignment
   D. say nothing to anyone about his complaint

In answering this question, you should study each of the choices to find which is best. Consider choice "A" – Certainly an employee may discuss his complaint with fellow employees, but no change or improvement can result, and the complaint remains unresolved. Choice "B" is a poor choice since the head of the organization probably does not know what assignment you have been given, and taking your problem to him is known as "going over the head" of the supervisor. The supervisor, or person who made the assignment, is the person who can clarify it or correct any injustice. Choice "C" is, therefore, correct. To say nothing, as in choice "D," is unwise. Supervisors have and interest in knowing the problems employees are facing, and the employee is seeking a solution to his problem.

2. True/False

3. Matching Questions
Matching an answer from a column of choices within another column.

V. RECORDING YOUR ANSWERS

Computer terminals are used more and more today for many different kinds of exams.

For an examination with very few applicants, you may be told to record your answers in the test booklet itself. Separate answer sheets are much more common. If this separate answer sheet is to be scored by machine – and this is often the case – it is highly important that you mark your answers correctly in order to get credit.

VI. BEFORE THE TEST

YOUR PHYSICAL CONDITION IS IMPORTANT
If you are not well, you can't do your best work on tests. If you are half asleep, you can't do your best either. Here are some tips:

1) Get about the same amount of sleep you usually get. Don't stay up all night before the test, either partying or worrying—DON'T DO IT!
2) If you wear glasses, be sure to wear them when you go to take the test. This goes for hearing aids, too.
3) If you have any physical problems that may keep you from doing your best, be sure to tell the person giving the test. If you are sick or in poor health, you relay cannot do your best on any test. You can always come back and take the test some other time.

Common sense will help you find procedures to follow to get ready for an examination. Too many of us, however, overlook these sensible measures. Indeed, nervousness and fatigue have been found to be the most serious reasons why applicants fail to do their best on civil service tests. Here is a list of reminders:

- Begin your preparation early – Don't wait until the last minute to go scurrying around for books and materials or to find out what the position is all about.
- Prepare continuously – An hour a night for a week is better than an all-night cram session. This has been definitely established. What is more, a night a week for a month will return better dividends than crowding your study into a shorter period of time.
- Locate the place of the exam – You have been sent a notice telling you when and where to report for the examination. If the location is in a different town or otherwise unfamiliar to you, it would be well to inquire the best route and learn something about the building.
- Relax the night before the test – Allow your mind to rest. Do not study at all that night. Plan some mild recreation or diversion; then go to bed early and get a good night's sleep.
- Get up early enough to make a leisurely trip to the place for the test – This way unforeseen events, traffic snarls, unfamiliar buildings, etc. will not upset you.

- Dress comfortably – A written test is not a fashion show. You will be known by number and not by name, so wear something comfortable.
- Leave excess paraphernalia at home – Shopping bags and odd bundles will get in your way. You need bring only the items mentioned in the official notice you received; usually everything you need is provided. Do not bring reference books to the exam. They will only confuse those last minutes and be taken away from you when in the test room.
- Arrive somewhat ahead of time – If because of transportation schedules you must get there very early, bring a newspaper or magazine to take your mind off yourself while waiting.
- Locate the examination room – When you have found the proper room, you will be directed to the seat or part of the room where you will sit. Sometimes you are given a sheet of instructions to read while you are waiting. Do not fill out any forms until you are told to do so; just read them and be prepared.
- Relax and prepare to listen to the instructions
- If you have any physical problem that may keep you from doing your best, be sure to tell the test administrator. If you are sick or in poor health, you really cannot do your best on the exam. You can come back and take the test some other time.

VII. AT THE TEST

The day of the test is here and you have the test booklet in your hand. The temptation to get going is very strong. Caution! There is more to success than knowing the right answers. You must know how to identify your papers and understand variations in the type of short-answer question used in this particular examination. Follow these suggestions for maximum results from your efforts:

1) Cooperate with the monitor
The test administrator has a duty to create a situation in which you can be as much at ease as possible. He will give instructions, tell you when to begin, check to see that you are marking your answer sheet correctly, and so on. He is not there to guard you, although he will see that your competitors do not take unfair advantage. He wants to help you do your best.

2) Listen to all instructions
Don't jump the gun! Wait until you understand all directions. In most civil service tests you get more time than you need to answer the questions. So don't be in a hurry. Read each word of instructions until you clearly understand the meaning. Study the examples, listen to all announcements and follow directions. Ask questions if you do not understand what to do.

3) Identify your papers
Civil service exams are usually identified by number only. You will be assigned a number; you must not put your name on your test papers. Be sure to copy your number correctly. Since more than one exam may be given, copy your exact examination title.

4) Plan your time
Unless you are told that a test is a "speed" or "rate of work" test, speed itself is usually not important. Time enough to answer all the questions will be provided, but this

does not mean that you have all day. An overall time limit has been set. Divide the total time (in minutes) by the number of questions to determine the approximate time you have for each question.

5) Do not linger over difficult questions

If you come across a difficult question, mark it with a paper clip (useful to have along) and come back to it when you have been through the booklet. One caution if you do this – be sure to skip a number on your answer sheet as well. Check often to be sure that you have not lost your place and that you are marking in the row numbered the same as the question you are answering.

6) Read the questions

Be sure you know what the question asks! Many capable people are unsuccessful because they failed to *read* the questions correctly.

7) Answer all questions

Unless you have been instructed that a penalty will be deducted for incorrect answers, it is better to guess than to omit a question.

8) Speed tests

It is often better NOT to guess on speed tests. It has been found that on timed tests people are tempted to spend the last few seconds before time is called in marking answers at random – without even reading them – in the hope of picking up a few extra points. To discourage this practice, the instructions may warn you that your score will be "corrected" for guessing. That is, a penalty will be applied. The incorrect answers will be deducted from the correct ones, or some other penalty formula will be used.

9) Review your answers

If you finish before time is called, go back to the questions you guessed or omitted to give them further thought. Review other answers if you have time.

10) Return your test materials

If you are ready to leave before others have finished or time is called, take ALL your materials to the monitor and leave quietly. Never take any test material with you. The monitor can discover whose papers are not complete, and taking a test booklet may be grounds for disqualification.

VIII. EXAMINATION TECHNIQUES

1) Read the general instructions carefully. These are usually printed on the first page of the exam booklet. As a rule, these instructions refer to the timing of the examination; the fact that you should not start work until the signal and must stop work at a signal, etc. If there are any *special* instructions, such as a choice of questions to be answered, make sure that you note this instruction carefully.

2) When you are ready to start work on the examination, that is as soon as the signal has been given, read the instructions to each question booklet, underline any key words or phrases, such as *least, best, outline, describe*

and the like. In this way you will tend to answer as requested rather than discover on reviewing your paper that you *listed without describing*, that you selected the *worst* choice rather than the *best* choice, etc.

3) If the examination is of the objective or multiple-choice type – that is, each question will also give a series of possible answers: A, B, C or D, and you are called upon to select the best answer and write the letter next to that answer on your answer paper – it is advisable to start answering each question in turn. There may be anywhere from 50 to 100 such questions in the three or four hours allotted and you can see how much time would be taken if you read through all the questions before beginning to answer any. Furthermore, if you come across a question or group of questions which you know would be difficult to answer, it would undoubtedly affect your handling of all the other questions.

4) If the examination is of the essay type and contains but a few questions, it is a moot point as to whether you should read all the questions before starting to answer any one. Of course, if you are given a choice – say five out of seven and the like – then it is essential to read all the questions so you can eliminate the two that are most difficult. If, however, you are asked to answer all the questions, there may be danger in trying to answer the easiest one first because you may find that you will spend too much time on it. The best technique is to answer the first question, then proceed to the second, etc.

5) Time your answers. Before the exam begins, write down the time it started, then add the time allowed for the examination and write down the time it must be completed, then divide the time available somewhat as follows:
    - If 3-1/2 hours are allowed, that would be 210 minutes. If you have 80 objective-type questions, that would be an average of 2-1/2 minutes per question. Allow yourself no more than 2 minutes per question, or a total of 160 minutes, which will permit about 50 minutes to review.
    - If for the time allotment of 210 minutes there are 7 essay questions to answer, that would average about 30 minutes a question. Give yourself only 25 minutes per question so that you have about 35 minutes to review.

6) The most important instruction is to *read each question* and make sure you know what is wanted. The second most important instruction is to *time yourself properly* so that you answer every question. The third most important instruction is to *answer every question*. Guess if you have to but include something for each question. Remember that you will receive no credit for a blank and will probably receive some credit if you write something in answer to an essay question. If you guess a letter – say "B" for a multiple-choice question – you may have guessed right. If you leave a blank as an answer to a multiple-choice question, the examiners may respect your feelings but it will not add a point to your score. Some exams may penalize you for wrong answers, so in such cases *only*, you may not want to guess unless you have some basis for your answer.

7) Suggestions
   a. Objective-type questions
      1. Examine the question booklet for proper sequence of pages and questions
      2. Read all instructions carefully
      3. Skip any question which seems too difficult; return to it after all other questions have been answered
      4. Apportion your time properly; do not spend too much time on any single question or group of questions
      5. Note and underline key words – *all, most, fewest, least, best, worst, same, opposite,* etc.
      6. Pay particular attention to negatives
      7. Note unusual option, e.g., unduly long, short, complex, different or similar in content to the body of the question
      8. Observe the use of "hedging" words – *probably, may, most likely,* etc.
      9. Make sure that your answer is put next to the same number as the question
      10. Do not second-guess unless you have good reason to believe the second answer is definitely more correct
      11. Cross out original answer if you decide another answer is more accurate; do not erase until you are ready to hand your paper in
      12. Answer all questions; guess unless instructed otherwise
      13. Leave time for review

   b. Essay questions
      1. Read each question carefully
      2. Determine exactly what is wanted. Underline key words or phrases.
      3. Decide on outline or paragraph answer
      4. Include many different points and elements unless asked to develop any one or two points or elements
      5. Show impartiality by giving pros and cons unless directed to select one side only
      6. Make and write down any assumptions you find necessary to answer the questions
      7. Watch your English, grammar, punctuation and choice of words
      8. Time your answers; don't crowd material

8) Answering the essay question

Most essay questions can be answered by framing the specific response around several key words or ideas. Here are a few such key words or ideas:

M's: manpower, materials, methods, money, management
P's: purpose, program, policy, plan, procedure, practice, problems, pitfalls, personnel, public relations
a. Six basic steps in handling problems:
   1. Preliminary plan and background development
   2. Collect information, data and facts
   3. Analyze and interpret information, data and facts
   4. Analyze and develop solutions as well as make recommendations

5. Prepare report and sell recommendations
6. Install recommendations and follow up effectiveness

b. Pitfalls to avoid
1. *Taking things for granted* – A statement of the situation does not necessarily imply that each of the elements is necessarily true; for example, a complaint may be invalid and biased so that all that can be taken for granted is that a complaint has been registered
2. *Considering only one side of a situation* – Wherever possible, indicate several alternatives and then point out the reasons you selected the best one
3. *Failing to indicate follow up* – Whenever your answer indicates action on your part, make certain that you will take proper follow-up action to see how successful your recommendations, procedures or actions turn out to be
4. *Taking too long in answering any single question* – Remember to time your answers properly

EXAMINATION SECTION

READING COMPREHENSION
COMMENTARY

Questions on reading comprehension – the ability to understand and interpret written materials – are now universal, staple parts of almost all aptitude and achievement tests, as well as tests of general and mental ability.

By its very nature, the reading comprehension question is the most difficult of the question-types to cope with successfully, and, accordingly, it is usually weighted more heavily (assigned more credits) than other questions.

Generally, tests of aptitude and/or achievement derive their reading selections ("passages") from the several disciplines – art, biology, chemistry, economics, education, engineering, history, literature, mathematics, music, philosophy, physics, political science, psychology, and sociology. Thus, the student or applicant is not being tested for specific knowledge of, or proficiency in, these areas. Rather, he is being tested on his understanding and comprehension of the meaning of the materials contained in the specific passages presented, the theory being that his mental ability will be best tested by his reading power, not by his training or acquired knowledge in the different fields, since it may be reasonably expected that such training and/or knowledge will differ among the candidates for a variety of reasons. The great equalizing element is the reading comprehension test. Therefore, all the information and material needed for answering the questions are imbedded in the passages themselves. *The power or skill or ability of the testtaker, then, is to be shown in the extent and degree to which he succeeds in making the correct answers to the questions in the reading passages.*

Historically, many colleges and universities, leaning on the theory of transfer of training, regard the reading comprehension factor as, perhaps the most important of all criteria in measuring scholastic aptitude since, according to this view, the ability to read with understanding and to go on from this point, is basic to all academic professional, graduate, and research work.

Let us examine just what reading comprehension means in the context described above and analyze its basic components.

The factor of reading ability is a complex one which may be tested and measured at several discrete levels of ability.

Comparatively, the easiest type of reading question is that which tests understanding of the material to be read – to list facts or details as described in the passage, to explain the meanings of words or phrases used, to clarify references, etc.

The next level of difficulty is reached when the student is confronted with questions designed to show his ability to interpret and to analyze the material to be read, e.g., to discover the central thought of the passage, to ascertain the mood or point of view of the author, to note contradictions, etc.

The third stage consists of the ability to apply the principles and/or opinions expressed in the article, e.g., to surmise the recommendations that the writer may be expected to make later on or to formulate his stand on related issues.

The final and highest point is attained when the student is called upon to evaluate what he has read – agree with or to differ with the point of view of the writer, to accept or to refute the evidences or methods employed, to judge the efficacy or the inappropriateness of different proposals, etc.

All these levels will be broached and tested in this reading section.

SAMPLE PASSAGE - QUESTIONS AND ANSWERS

PASSAGE

(1) Our ignorance of the complex subject of social insurance was and remains colossal. (2) For years American business leaders delighted in maligning the British social insurance schemes. (3) Our industrialists condemned them without ever finding out what they were about. (4) Even our universities displayed no interest. (5) Contrary to the interest in this subject taken by organized labor abroad, our own labor movement bitterly opposed the entire program of social insurance up to a few years ago. (6) Since the success of any reform depends largely upon a correct public understanding of the principles involved, the adoption of social insurance measures presented peculiar difficulties for the United States under our Federal type of government of limited powers, our constitutional and judicial handicaps, our long conditioning to individualism, the traditional hostility to social reform by both capital and labor, the general inertia, and our complete lack of trained administrative personnel without which even the best law can be ineffective. (7) Has not bitter experience taught us that far more important than the passage of a law, which is at best only a declaration of intention, is a ready public opinion prepared to enforce it?

1. According to this writer, what attitude have we shown in this country toward social insurance?   1.__

    A. We have been extremely doubtful that it will work, but have been willing to give it a chance.
    B. We have opposed it on the grounds of a careful study of its defects.
    C. We have shown an unintelligent and rather blind antagonism toward it.
    D. We have been afraid that it would not work under our type of government.
    E. We have resented it because of the extensive propaganda in favor of it.

2. To what does the phrase, "our long conditioning to individualism," refer?   2.__

    A. Our habit of depending upon ourselves
    B. Our increasing dependence on the Federal Government
    C. Our long established distrust of "big business"
    D. Our policies of high protective tariff
    E. Our unwillingness to accept reforms

3. Which of these ideas is expressed in this passage?   3.____

   A. The surest way to cure a social evil is to get people to pass a law against it.
   B. Legislation alone cannot effect social reforms.
   C. The American people are seriously uninformed about all social problems.
   D. Our type of government makes social reform practically impossible.
   E. Capital and labor retard social progress.

ANALYSIS

These are the steps you must take to answer the questions:

First, scan the passage quickly, trying to gather at a glance the general import.

Then, read the passage carefully and critically, underlining with a pencil, what are apparently leading phrases and concepts.

Next, read each question carefully, and seek the answer in definite parts – sentences, clauses, phrases, figures of speech, adverbs, adjectives, etc. – in the text of the passage.

Finally, select the one answer which best answers the question, that is, it *best* matches what the paragraph says or is *best* supported by something in the passage.

The passage is concerned with the advent of social insurance to the United States. The author makes several points in this connection:

1. Our gross ignorance of, and lack of interest in, the subject.
2. The bitter opposition to social insurance in this country, particularly, of organized labor.
3. Special and augmented difficulties in the United States in respect to this area; enumeration of these factors.
4. The ultimate, certain method of achieving reform.

Having firmly encompassed the central meaning and basic contents of the passage, let us now proceed to examine each of the stated questions and proposed answers.

Question 1.   According to this writer, what attitude have we shown in this country toward social insurance?

   A. We have been extremely doubtful that it will work, but have been willing to give it a chance.
      Sentences 1, 2, 3, 4, 5 drastically negate the second clause of this statement ("but we have been willing to give it a chance").
   B. We have opposed it on the grounds of a careful study of its defects.
      This statement is completely refuted by sentences 2 and 3.
   C. We have shown an unintelligent and rather blind antagonism toward it.
      Just as A is fully denied by sentences 1-5, so these sentences fully Affirm the validity of this statement.
   D. We have been afraid that it would not work under our type of government.
      This is one – and only one – of the several difficulties facing the success of social insurance. Thus, this answer is only *partially* true.
   E. We have resented it because of the extensive propaganda in favor of it.
      Quite the contrary. Again, see sentences 1-5.

Looking back, you now see that the one suggested answer of the five (5) offered that BEST answers the question is item C, We have shown an unintelligent and rather blind antagonism toward it. The CORRECT answer, then, is C.

Question 2.   To what does the phrase, "our long conditioning to individualism," refer?
   A.   Our habit of depending upon ourselves.
         When a phrase is quoted from the text, as in this question, we should immediately locate it, review the context, and then consider it *in the light of the meaning of the passage as a whole.*
         We find the quoted phrase in long sentence 6, beginning "Since the success..."
         A is clearly the answer to question 2.
   Items B, C, D, E have little or no merit with reference to the meaning of the quoted phrase within the passage, and are, therefore, to be discarded as possible answers.

Question 3.   Which of these ideas is expressed in this passage?
   A.   The surest way to cure a social evil is to get people to pass a law against it.
         This is clearly refuted by the last sentence, "Has not bitter experience... it?"
   B.   Legislation alone cannot effect social reforms.
         This is just as clearly supported by this same last sentence.
   C.   The American people are seriously uninformed about all social problems.
      There is no evidence in the passage to support this statement.
   D.   Our type of government makes social reform practically impossible.
         Our democratic form of government does present serious handicaps to social reform, as stated in the next-to-last sentence, but does not make social reform "practically impossible."
   E.   Capital and labor retard social progress.
         American business leaders and the labor movement both opposed social *insurance.* They did not, however, retard social *progress.*

———

SUGGESTIONS FOR ANSWERING THE READING COMPREHENSION QUESTION

1. Be sure to answer the questions only on the basis of the passage, and not from any other source, unless specifically directed to do otherwise.

2. Note that the answers may not be found directly in the text. For the more difficult reading questions, answers are generally to be *inferred* or *derived* from the sense of one or more sentences, clauses, and even paragraphs.

3. Do not expect to find the bases for the answers in sequential parts of the textual material. The difficulty of questions is increased when the candidate is required to skip from one part of the passage to another without any order, i.e., Question 1 may have its root in the last sentence of the paragraph, let us say, and Question 5 may be based upon the second sentence, for example. This is a method of increasing the difficulty of the research and investigation required of the candidate.

4. When the question refers to a specific line, sentence, paragraph, or quotation, be sure to find this reference and to re-read it thoroughly. The answer to such a question is almost certain to be found in or near this reference in the passage.

5. Time for the reading question is limited, as it is for the examination as a whole. In other words, one must work speedily as well as effectively. The candidate, in seeking the answers to the reading questions, is not expected to go through all of the items in the thorough way presented in the sample questions above. That is, he has only to suit himself. It suffices, in order to attain to the right answer, to note mentally the basis for the answer in the text. There is no need to annotate your answer or to write out reasons for your answer. What we have attempted to do in the samples is to show that there is a definite and logical attack on this type of question, which, principally, consists of careful, critical reading, research and investigation, and evaluation of the material. One must learn to arrive at the correct answer through this process rather than through hit-or-miss tactics or guessing. There is no reading comprehension question, logically or fairly devised, which cannot be answered by the candidate provided he goes about this task in a systematic, sustained manner.

6. The candidate may be assisted by this advanced technique. Often, the general sense of the passage when fully captured, rather than specific parts in the passage, will lead to the correct answer. Therefore, it is most important that the candidate read the passage for total meaning first. This type of general understanding will be most helpful in answering those questions which have no specific background in the text but, rather, must be inferred from what has been read.

7. Beware of the following pitfalls:
    A. The categorical statement. – You can almost be sure that any answer which uses the words solely, wholly, always, never, at all times, forever, etc., is wrong.
    B. The too-easy answer. – When the question appears to be so simple that it can be answered almost word for word by reference to the text, be particularly on your guard. You will, probably, find that the language of the question may have been inverted or changed or that some important word has been added or omitted, so that you are being tested for alertness and attention to details. For example, if, in a passage, a comparison is made between Country A and Country B, and you are told that Country A has twice the area of Country B, and the question contains an item which states that "it is clear that the area of Country B is

greater than Country A," note how easily you can be beguiled into accepting this statement as true.

     C.   Questions requiring that the candidate show his understanding of the main point of a passage, e.g., to state the central theme, or to suggest a worthy title, must be answered on that basis alone. You may be sure that other worthy possibilities are available, but you should examine your choice from the points of view of both appropriateness and breadth. For the most part, answers that are ruled out will contain one, but not both of these characteristics.

     D.   Make up your mind now that some, but not all, of the material in the various passages in the reading comprehension questions will be useful for finding the answer. Sometimes, passages are made purposely long to increase the difficulty and to further confuse the harried candidates. However, do not disregard any of the textual material without first having given it a thorough reading.

     E.   If the question requires that you give the writer's opinion or feelings on possible future action, do just that, and do not substitute your own predilections or antidotes. Similarly, do not make inferences if there exists in the text a clear-cut statement of facts. Base your answer, preferably, on the facts; make inferences or assumptions when they are called for, or as necessary.

     F.   Do not expect the passages to deal with your subject field(s) alone. The passages offered will illustrate all the academic areas. While interest is a major factor in attaining to success, resolve now that you are going to wade through all the passages, in a thorough way, be they science or mathematics or economics or art. Unfamiliarity with a subject is no excuse on this type of test since the answers are to be based upon the reading passage underline.

     In corollary fashion, should you encounter a passage dealing with a field with which you are familiar, do not permit your special knowledge to play a part in your answer. Answer _only_ on the basis of the passage, as _directed_.

     G.   The hardest type of reading question is the one in which the fifth choice presented is "none of these." Should this phrase prove to be the correct answer, it would require a thorough, albeit rapid, examination of ALL the possibilities. This, of course, is time consuming and often frustrating.

     H.   A final word of advice at this point. On the examination, leave the more difficult reading questions for the end. Try to answer those of lesser difficulty first. In this way, you will leave yourself maximum time for the _really_ difficult part of the examination.

     In accordance with the special challenge of the reading comprehension question, ten (10) selected passages, varying in subject matter, style, length, and form, are presented for solution by the candidate. However, the passages are all alike in one respect: they extend to the highest ranges of difficulty.

READING COMPREHENSION
SAMPLE QUESTIONS WITH ANSWERS AND EXPLANATIONS

FORM A

Many jobs require the ability to analyze, understand, and interpret written material of varying levels of complexity and to retain the content for at least a limited period of time.

This question type is primarily designed to test these comprehension and retention abilities. The following questions, therefore, require competitors to understand a given paragraph and to select an answer based on their comprehension of the conceptual content of the paragraph.

The right answer is either (1) a repetition, formulated in different terminology, of the main concept or concepts found in the paragraph, or (2) a conclusion whose inherence in the content of the paragraph is such that it is equivalent to a restatement.

1. Through advertising, manufacturers exercise a high degree of control over consumers' desires. However, the manufacturer assumes enormous risks in attempting to predict what consumers will want and in producing goods in quantity and distributing them in advance of final selection by the consumers.
   The paragraph BEST supports the statement that manufacturers

   A. can eliminate the risk of overproduction by advertising
   B. completely control buyers' needs and desires
   C. must depend upon the final consumers for the success of their undertakings
   D. distribute goods directly to the consumers
   E. can predict with great accuracy the success of any product they put on the market

1.____

The conclusion derived by the correct alternative, C, is inherent in the content of the paragraph; although it acknowledges that advertising plays an important role in determining consumers' desires, it affirms that final selection rests with the consumers and that manufacturers, therefore, take enormous risks in attempting to predict final selection.

Alternative B contradicts the opening sentence of the paragraph which refers only to a *high degree of control.*

Alternatives A and E likewise affirm the opposite of what the paragraph postulates, i.e., that the manufacturer's predictions entail enormous risks.

Alternative D is almost irrelevant to the paragraph since distribution techniques have not been considered.

2. The function of business is to increase the wealth of the country and the value and happiness of life. It does this by supplying the material needs of men and women. When the nation's business is successfully carried on, it renders public service of the highest value.
   The paragraph BEST supports the statement that

   A. all businesses which render public service are successful
   B. human happiness is enhanced only by the increase of material wants
   C. the value of life is increased only by the increase of wealth
   D. the material needs of men and women are supplied by well-conducted business
   E. business is the only field of activity which increases happiness

2.____

The correct alternative, D, restates the main idea in the original paragraph that business increases the value and happiness of life by supplying the material needs of men and women.

Alternative A derives its conclusion incorrectly, i.e., the proposition that all successful businesses render public service, cannot be logically reversed to *all businesses which render public service are successful.*

Alternatives B and C assume an equation between happiness and wealth which is not supported by the content of the paragraph.

Alternative E likewise equates happiness with business endeavors or their products, which the content of the paragraph does not warrant.

3. Honest people in one nation find it difficult to understand the viewpoints of honest people in another. Foreign ministries and their ministers exist for the purpose of explaining the viewpoints of one nation in terms understood by the ministries of another. Some of their most important work lies in this direction. The paragraph BEST supports the statement that

    A. people of different nations may not consider matters in the same light
    B. it is unusual for many people to share similar ideas
    C. suspicion prevents understanding between nations
    D. the chief work of foreign ministries is to guide relations between nations united by a common cause
    E. the people of one nation must sympathize with the viewpoints of the people of other nations

3.____

The conclusion derived by the correct alternative, A, is inherent in the content of the paragraph; if honest people in one nation find it difficult to understand the viewpoints of honest people in another, it is because they often see matters in different lights.

Alternatives B, C, and D find little or no support in the paragraph; B is concerned with *many people* whereas the paragraph refers to people of different nations; C assumes that nations are suspicious of each other and that suspicion prevents understanding; D contradicts the main idea expressed by the paragraph since foreign ministries should work towards mutual understanding between nations having discrepant viewpoints whether or not they have a common cause.

Alternative E sets forth an ethical command which to an extent stems from the content of the paragraph but which is not completely warranted by it as is the conclusion of alternative

4. Education should not stop when the individual has been prepared to make a livelihood and to live in modern society. Living would be mere existence were there no appreciation and enjoyment of the riches of art, literature, and science. The paragraph BEST supports the statement that true education

    A. is focused on the routine problems of life
    B. prepares one for a full enjoyment of life
    C. deals chiefly with art, literature, and science
    D. is not possible for one who does not enjoy scientific literature
    E. disregards practical ends

4.___

The correct alternative, B, restates the main idea presented in the paragraph that living is mere existence for those individuals who lack the enjoyment of art, literature, and science.

Alternative A directly contradicts this main idea, and alternatives C and E also contradict the paragraph which acknowledges that education should prepare the individual to make a livelihood although it shouldn't stop there.

Alternative D goes beyond the paragraph in that it affirms that each individual must enjoy scientific literature, whereas the original statement simply suggests that life in general would be limited if the riches of science, art, and literature were not available for appreciation and enjoyment.

———

4

FORM B

The development of plans, systems, and procedures is an essential function of many jobs. This function entails the ability to analyze given facts and discover their implications, as well as the ability to reason from general principles to the implications of these principles in specific situations.

Question-type B tests these analytical abilities.

Accordingly, each of the following questions consists of a statement which is to be accepted as true and should not be questioned for the purpose of this test. Following the statement are five alternatives. The correct alternative MUST derive from the information given in the original statement without drawing on additional information. By contrast, the four incorrect alternatives rest, to varying degrees, on the admission of new information.

1. No substantial alterations in the age structure took place between 1960-70, and life expectancy remained the same. A slight drop, nonetheless (from 38 to 37 percent), is noted in the proportion of the population 20 years of age and younger. Therefore, between 1960-70,

    A. the proportion of the productive-age population increased
    B. there was a slight decrease in fertility rates
    C. there was a decrease in emigration
    D. there was a slight increase in infant mortality
    E. production remained substantially the same

    1.____

The correct alternative, A, follows from the data that there was a slight drop in the proportion of the population under 20 years of age and that life expectancy remained the same.

Alternatives B and D are possible explanations of the slight decrease in the proportion of the younger population but do not derive from the original statement and would require additional evidence.

Alternative C would likewise require additional information and would seem to apply more as a partial and possible explanation of a decrease in the productive-age population.

Alternative E in no way derives from the given data since many factors affect production besides the age structure of the population.

2. A robot can take a walk in order to mail a letter; it can play chess, build other machines, and generally exhibit rule-governed behavior. A robot can kill a person but, unlike a person, it cannot be ashamed. It can be annoying but not annoyed. It can *perhaps* exhibit behavior as *if* it were ashamed or annoyed.

    A. Robots are capable of thought.
    B. Robots can do things that people do but cannot be what people are.
    C. Robots and people are outwardly the same.
    D. Robots can make conscious decisions but have no moral consciousness.
    E. Robots never exhibit their inner thoughts and realities.

    2.____

The correct alternative, B, derives its conclusion from the joint consideration of the actions enumerated in the original statement as actions that a robot can perform – mailing a letter, playing chess, killing a person – and the conscious states that are enumerated as impossible in a robot, i.e., being ashamed or annoyed. Furthermore, the last sentence in the original statement contrasts outward behaviors with the actual conscious states they represent.

Alternative A rests on the assumption that thought can be equated with exhibited behavior and not with inner consciousness.

Alternative C assumes not only that all exhibited behavior is the same but that the outward appearance of a robot and a person is the same.

Alternative D correctly derives a section of its conclusion–the lack of moral consciousness – from the stated fact that a robot cannot be ashamed, but assumes that a robot can kill a person after making a conscious decision, which contradicts the original statement.

Alternative E likewise affirms, in contradiction of the original statement, that robots have inner consciousness.

3.   The Thirty Years' War, 1618 to 1648, established the principle of religious toleration among the German states, but it also reduced the German population by at least one-third, and much of the cultivated land became wilderness. Therefore, the Thirty Years' War   3.____

    A.   altered the geographical boundaries of the German states
    B.   was generally beneficial to the German states
    C.   was fought on German soil
    D.   established a large number of religions within the German states
    E.   caused the German population to become widely scattered

The correct alternative, C, derives its conclusion from the given facts that the German population was reduced by one-third and much of the cultivated land became wilderness.

Alternative A, on the other hand, assumes the establishment of new borders from the extraneous information that borders are usually changed by wars.

Alternative B derives its conclusion from the assumption that religious tolerance creates a surrounding influence beneficial to all aspects of national life.

Alternative D assumes an equation between religious tolerance and religious pluralism, and alternative E likewise assumes an equation between the reduction of the population and the scattering of the population.

4.   Though easy to learn, backgammon is a surprisingly subtle and complex game to play very well. It is a game that calls for mastery of the laws of probability and the ability to weigh and undertake frequent shifts in strategy. Therefore, a necessary quality for playing backgammon very well is   4.____

A. the ability to deceive the opponent
B. a willingness to take calculated risks
C. a high degree of manual dexterity
D. the ability to make quick decisions
E. a mastery of advanced mathematics

The correct alternative, B, derives its conclusion from the given fact that the game is based on decisions of probability. Thus, the player must take calculated risks.

The four incorrect alternatives, on the other hand, rest on assumptions that, to varying degrees, go beyond the original statement. Alternative E, for example, assumes that a mastery of the laws of probability entails a more generic mastery of advanced mathematics. Alternative D assumes that frequent shifts in strategy cannot be carried out slowly.

———

FORM C

Many jobs require the ability to solve a presented problem when all the necessary facts to solve the problem are not given.

Solution to the problem involves making some reasonable assumptions or anticipating what the most likely of several possible occurrences might be. This ability becomes especially important when decisions must be reached based on incomplete evidence. Accordingly, the questions in this section require competitors to select the best or most reasonable answer from five alternatives.

In order to do so, competitors are required to use general knowledge not included in the original statement. Since the correct alternative consists of the best or most reasonable answer, it is essential to keep in mind that some alternatives may be plausible as the correct alternative.

1. The development of a country's water power is advocated as a means of conserving nat-   1.____
    ural resources CHIEFLY because such a hydroelectric policy would tend to

    A. stimulate the growth of industries in hitherto isolated regions
    B. encourage the substitution of machinery for hand labor
    C. provide a larger market for coal
    D. make cheap electricity available in rural areas
    E. lessen the use of irreplaceable fuel materials

Of the five alternatives, the correct alternative, E, derives from the fundamental or most essential reason for the endorsement of a hydroelectric policy, i.e., water is not a depletable energy resource.

Alternatives A and D are plausible but are not as determinative as E.

Alternative C is easily discarded since coal would have a larger market in the absence of hydroelectric power.

Alternative B is also easily discarded since hydroelectric energy would increase the availability of both the fuel and/or electricity needed to run machinery.

2. Complaints by the owners of large cars that they cannot see an already-parked small car   2.____
    in a parking lot until they have begun to pull into a space are BEST justified if

    A. there are few empty parking spaces in the lot
    B. the small car has been parked for a long time
    C. the owners of large cars have poor vision
    D. there is a designated parking area for small cars
    E. there are few other small cars in the lot

The correct alternative, D, hinges on the fact that strict *justification* for a complaint is more firmly rooted in legality than in individual situations or attitudes.

Thus, for example, the owner of a large car who happens to find few empty parking spaces in a lot (alternative A), or who knows or assumes that a small car has been parked in a certain space for a long time (alternative B), can justify his or her annoyance only on the subjective level. On the other hand, if a small car is parked in a space designated for large cars, the individual's annoyance and complaint acquire objective and formal justification.

3. A country that is newly settled usually produces very little art, music, or literature. The MOST REASONABLE explanation of this fact is that   3.____

    A. its people have had few experiences to draw on
    B. there is little use for such work
    C. suitable materials for such work must be imported
    D. the physical development of the country absorbs most of the interest and energy of the people
    E. there is as yet no governmental encouragement of the arts

The correct alternative, D, presents the most basic explanation for the lack of artistic production in a newly-settled country. The development of a newly-settled country necessitates the undivided attention of its people, and manpower is thus basically unavailable for the production of art, music, or literature.

Alternative A is implausible since newly-settled people have many experiences which are eventually represented in the art, music, and literature of later generations.

Alternatives B, C, and E make assumptions about conditions necessary for the production of art, music, and literature which are only partially valid.

Alternative B incorrectly assumes that art is always produced for utilitarian purposes.

Alternative C partially applies to art and music but not at all to literature.

Alternative E is only partially plausible. The government of a newly-settled country is likely to encourage the production of goods rather than the production of art, music, or literature. However, artistic production can occur without governmental encouragement.

4. The CHIEF reason why every society has certain words and concepts that are never precisely translated into the language of another society is that   4.___

    A. the art of good translation is as yet not sufficiently developed
    B. there is too great a disparity between the intellectual levels attained by different societies
    C. every society possesses cultural elements which are unique to itself
    D. words and concepts never express the true nature of a society
    E. every society has some ideas which it does not wish to share with other societies

The correct alternative, C, is the most basic reason why certain concepts are never precisely translated. Languages express the sociopolitical contexts in which they are spoken and are bound to have expressions that are unique to these contexts.

Alternative A fails to distinguish between the qualitative and the quantitative. Whereas the art of good translation appears to be as yet not sufficiently widespread, it is indeed available.

Furthermore, its total unavailability would still constitute a secondary explanation, over and against alternative C, for the impossibility of the precise translation of certain words.

Alternative B rests on the assumption that *all* existing societies are substantially disparate in their level of development, which is known not to be the case.

Alternative D assumes the truth of the postulate expounded by some philosophical theories that words and concepts have no referential value.

Alternative E presents a farfetched ethical judgment whose plausibility rests on the assumption that social groups are secretive and that the function of language is to exclude communication beyond the social group.

———

READING COMPREHENSION
UNDERSTANDING AND INTERPRETING WRITTEN MATERIAL
STRATEGIES

Surveying Passages, Sentences as Cues

While individual readers develop unique reading styles and skills, there are some known strategies which can assist any reader in improving his or her reading comprehension and performance on the reading subtest. These strategies include understanding how single paragraphs and entire passages are structured, how the ideas in them are ordered, and how the author of the passage has connected these ideas in a logical and sequential way for the reader.

The section that follows highlights the importance of reading a passage through once for meaning, and provides instruction on careful reading for context cues within the sentences before and after the missing word.

SURVEY THE ENTIRE PASSAGE

To get a sense of the topic and the organization of ideas in a passage, it is important to survey each passage initially in its entirety and to identify the main idea. (The first sentence of a paragraph usually states the main idea.) Do not try to fill in the blanks initially. The purpose of surveying a passage is to prepare for the more careful reading which will follow. You need a sense of the big picture before you start to fill in the details; for example, a quick survey of the passage on page 11, indicates that the topic is the early history of universities. The paragraphs are organized to provide information on the origin of the first universities, the associations formed by teachers and students, the early curriculum, and graduation requirements.

READ PRECEDING SENTENCES CAREFULLY

The missing words in a passage cannot be determined by reading and understanding only the sentences in which the deletions occur. Information from the sentences which precede or follow can provide important cues to determine the correct choice. For example, if you read the first sentence from the passage about universities which contains a blank, you will notice that all the alternatives make sense if this one sentence is read in isolation:

Nobody actually _____ them.

A.	started	B.	guarded
C.	blamed	D.	compared
E.	remembered		

The only way that you can make the correct word choice is to read the preceding sentences. In the excerpt below, notice that the first sentence tells the reader what the passage will be about: how universities developed. A key word in the first sentence is *emerged*, which is closely related in meaning to one of the five choices for the first blank. The second sentence explains the key word, *emerged*, by pointing out that we have no historical record of a decree or a date indicating when the first university was established. Understanding the ideas in the first two sentences makes it possible to select the correct word for the blank. Look at the sentence with the deleted word in the context of the preceding sentences and think about why you are now able to make the correct choice.

The first universities emerged at the end of the 11th century and beginning of the 12th. These institutions were not founded on any particular date or created by any formal action. Nobody actually _____ them.

A. started
C. blamed
E. remembered

B. guarded
D. compared

Started is the best choice because it fits the main idea of the passage and is closely related to the key word *emerged.*

READ THE SENTENCE WHICH FOLLOWS TO VERIFY YOUR CHOICE

The sentences which follow the one from which a word has been deleted may also provide cues to the correct choice. For example, look at an excerpt from the passage about universities again, and consider how the sentence which follows the one with the blank helps to reinforce the choice of the word, *started.*

The first universities emerged at the end of the llth century and the beginning of the 12th. These institutions were not founded on any particular date or created by any formal action. Nobody actually _____ them. Instead, they developed gradually in places like Paris, Oxford, and Bologna, where scholars had long been teaching students.

A. started
C. blamed
E. remembered

B. guarded
D. compared

The words, *developed gradually,* mean the same as the key word, *emerged.* The signal word, *instead,* helps to distinguish the difference between starting on a specific date as a result of some particular act or event and emerging over a period of time as a result of various factors.

Here is another example of how the sentence which follows the one from which a word is deleted might help you decide which of two good alternatives is the correct choice. This excerpt is from the practice passage about bridges (page 11).

Bridges are built to allow a continuous flow of highway and railway traffic across water lying in their paths. But engineers cannot forget that river traffic, too, is essential to our economy. The role of _____ is important. To keep these vessels moving freely, bridges are built big enough, when possible, to let them pass underneath.

A. wind
C. weight
E. experiences

B. boats
D. wires

After the first two sentences, the reader may be uncertain about the direction the writer intended to take in the rest of the paragraph. If the writer intended to continue the paragraph with information concerning how engineers make choices about the relative importance and requirements of land traffic and river traffic, *experience* might be the appropriate choice for the missing word. However, the sentence following the one in which the deletion occurs makes it clear that *boats* is the correct choice. It provides the synonym *vessels,* which in the noun phrase *these vessels* must refer back to the previous sentence or sentences. The phrase *to let them pass underneath* also helps make it clear that *boats* is the appropriate choice. *Them* refers back to *these vessels* which, in turn, refers back to *boats* when the word *boats* is placed in the previous sentence. Thus, the reader may use these cohesive ties (the pronoun referents) to verify the final choice.

Even when the text following a sentence with a deletion is not necessary to choose the best alternative, it may be helpful in other ways. Specifically, complete sentences provide important transitions into a related topic which is developed in the rest of the paragraph or in the next paragraph of the same passage. For example, the first paragraph in the passage about universities ends with a sentence which introduces the term *guilds*: *But, over time, they joined together to form guilds.* Prior to this sentence, information about the slow emergence of universities and about how independently scholars had acted was introduced. The next paragraph begins with two sentences about guilds in general. Someone who had not read the last sentence in the first paragraph might have missed the link between guilds and scholars and universities and, thus, might have been unnecessarily confused.

Cohesive Ties As Cues

Sentences in a paragraph may be linked together by several devices called cohesive ties. Attention to these ties may provide further cues about missing words. This section will describe the different types of cohesive ties and show how attention to them can help you to select the correct word.

PERSONAL PRONOUNS

Personal pronouns (e.g., he, she, they, it, its) are often used in adjoining sentences to refer back to an already mentioned person, place, thing, or idea. The word to which the pronoun refers is called the antecedent.

Tools used in farm work changed very slowly from ancient times to the eighteenth century, and the changes were minor. Since the eighteenth century *they* have changed quickly and dramatically.

The word *they* refers back to *tools* in the example above.

In the examination reading subtest, a deleted word sometimes occurs in a sentence in which the sentence subject is a pronoun that refers back to a previously mentioned noun. You must correctly identify the referent for the particular pronoun in order to interpret the sentence and select the correct answer. Here is an example from the passage about bridges.

An ingenious engineer designed the bridge so that it did not have to be raised above traffic. Instead it was _____.

A. burned
C. secured
E. lowered

B. emptied
D. shared

Q. What is the antecedent of *it* in both cases in the example?

A. The antecedent, of course, is *bridge*.

DEMONSTRATIVE PRONOUNS

Demonstrative pronouns (e.g., this, that, these) are also used to refer to a specific, previously mentioned noun. They may occur alone as noun replacements, or they may accompany and modify nouns.

I like jogging, swimming, and tennis. *These* are the only sports I enjoy.

In the sentence above, the word *these* is a replacement noun. However, demonstrative pronouns may also occur as adjectives modifying nouns.

I like jogging, swimming, and tennis. *These* sports are the only ones I enjoy.

The word *these* in the example above is an adjective modifier. The word *these* in each of the two previous examples refers to *jogging, swimming,* and *tennis.*

Here is an example from the passage about universities on page 12.

Undergraduates took classes in Greek philosophy, Latin grammar, arithmetic, music, and astronomy. These were the only _____ available.

A. rooms B. subjects
C. clothes D. pens
E. company

Q. Which word is a noun replacement?
A. The word *these* is the replacement noun for *Greek philosophy, Latin grammar, arithmetic, music,* and *astronomy.*

Here is another example from the same passage.

The concept of a fixed program of study leading to a degree first evolved in Medieval Europe. This _____ had not appeared before.

A. idea B. desk
C. library D. capital

Q. What is the antecedent of *this*?

A. The antecedent is *the concept of a fixed program of study leading to a degree.*

COMPARATIVE ADJECTIVES AND ADVERBS

When comparative adjectives or adverbs (e.g., so, such, better, more) occur, they refer to something else in the passage, otherwise a comparison could not be made.

The hotels in the city were all full; so were the motels and boarding houses.

Q. To what in the first sentence does the word *so* refer?
A. *So* tells us to compare the *motels* and *boarding houses* to the *hotels in the city.*

Q. In what way are the *hotels, motels,* and *boarding houses* similar to each other?

5

A. The *hotels, motels,* and *boarding houses* are similar in that they were all *full.*

Look at an example from the passage about universities.

Guilds were groups of tradespeople, somewhat akin to modern trade unions. In the Middle Ages, all the crafts had such

    A. taxes   B. secrets
    C. products   D. problems
    E. organizations

Q. To what in the first sentence does the word *such* refer?
A. *Such* refers to *groups of tradespeople.*

SUBSTITUTIONS

Substitution is another form of cohesive tie. A substitution occurs when one linguistic item (e.g., a noun) is replaced by another. Sometimes the substitution provides new or contrasting information. The substitution is not identical to the original, or antecedent, idea. A frequently occurring substitution involves the use of *one.* A noun substitution may involve another member of the same class as the original one.

My car is falling apart. I need a new one.

Q. What in the first sentence is replaced in the second sentence with *one?*
A. *One* is a substitute for the specific car mentioned in the first sentence. The contrast comes from the fact that the *new one* isn't the writer's current car.

The substitution may also pinpoint a specific member of a general class.

1. There are many unusual courses available at the university this summer. The *one* I am taking is called *Death and Dying.*
2. There are many unusual courses available at the university this summer. *Some* have never been offered before.

Q. In these examples, what is the general class in the first sentence that is replaced by *one* and by *some?*
A. In both cases the words *one* and *some* replace *many unusual* courses.

SYNONYMS

Synonyms are words that have similar meaning. In the examination reading subtest, a synonym of a deleted word is sometimes found in one of the sentences before and/or after the sentence with the deletion. Examine the following excerpt from the passage about bridges again.

But engineers cannot forget that river traffic, too, is essential to our economy. The role of _____ is important. To keep these vessels moving freely, bridges are built high enough, when possible, to let them pass underneath.

A. wind	B. boats
C. weight	D. wires
E. experience	

Q   Can you identify synonyms in the sentences, before and after the sentence containing the deletion, which are cues to the correct deleted word?

A.   If you identified the correct words, you probably noticed that *river traffic* is not exactly a synonym, since it is a slightly more general term than the word *boats* (the correct choice). But the word *vessels* is a direct synonym. Demonstrative pronouns (this, that, these, those) are sometimes used as modifiers for synonymous nouns in sentences which follow those containing deletions. The word *these* in *these vessels* is the demonstrative pronoun (modifier) for the synonymous noun *vessels*.

ANTONYMS

Antonyms are words of opposite meaning. In the examination reading subtest passages, antonyms may be cues for missing words. A contrasting relationship, which calls for the use of an antonym, is often signaled by the connective words *instead, however, but,* etc. Look at an excerpt from the passage about bridges.

An ingenious engineer designed the bridge so that it did not have to be raised above traffic. Instead it was _____.

A. burned	B. emptied
C. secured	D. shared
E. lowered	

Q.   Can you identify an antonym in the first sentence for one of the five alternatives?
A.   The word *raised* is an antonym for the word *lowered*.

SUPERORDINATE-SUBORDINATE WORDS

In the examination reading subtest, a passage sometimes contains a general term which provides a cue that a more specific term is the appropriate alternative. At other times, the passage may contain a specific term which provides cues that a general term is the appropriate alternative for a particular deletion. The general and more specific words are said to have superordinate-subordinate relationships.

Look at example 1 below. The more specific word *boy* in the first sentence serves as the antecedent for the more general word *child* in the second sentence. In example 2, the relationship is reversed. In both examples, the words *child* and *boy* reflect a superordinate-subordinate relationship.
1.   The *boy* climbed the tree. Then the *child* fell.
2.   The *child* climbed the tree. Then the *boy* fell.

In the practice passage about bridges on page 11, the phrase *river traffic* is a general term that is superordinate to the alternative *boats* (item 1). Later in the passage about bridges the following sentences also contain superordinate-subordinate words:

A lift bridge was desired, but there were wartime shortages of steel and machinery needed for the towers. It was hard to find enough _____.

A. work
C. time
E. space

B. material
D. power

Q. Can you identify two words in the first sentence that are specific examples for the correct response in the second sentence?
A. Of course, the words *steel* and *machinery* are the specific examples for the more general term *material.*

WORDS ASSOCIATED BY ENTAILMENT

Sometimes the concept described by one word within the context of the passage entails, or implies, the concept described by another word. For example, consider again item 7 in the practice passage about bridges. Notice how the follow-up sentence to item 7 provides a cue to the correct response.

An ingenious engineer designed the bridge so that it did not have to be raised above traffic. Instead it was _____. It could be submerged seven meters below the surface of the river.

A. burned
C. secured
E. lowered

B. emptied
D. shared

Q. What word in the sentence after the blank implies the concept of an alternative?
A. *Submerged* implies *lowered.* The concept of submerging something implies the idea of lowering the object beneath the surface of the water.

WORDS ASSOCIATED BY PART-WHOLE RELATIONSHIPS

Words may be related because they involve part of a whole and the whole itself; for example, *nose* and *face.* Words may also be related because they involve two parts of the same whole; for example, *radiator* and *muffler* both refer to parts of a car.

The captain of the ship was nervous. The storm was becoming worse and worse. The hardened man paced the _____.

A. floor
C. deck

B. hall
D. court

Q. Which choice has a part-whole relationship with a word in the sentences above?
A. A *deck* is a part of a *ship.* Therefore, *deck* has a part-whole relationship with *ship.*

CONJUNCTIVE AND CONNECTIVE WORDS AND PHRASES

Conjunctions or connectives are words or phrases that connect parts of sentences or parts of a passage to each other. Their purpose is to help the reader understand the logical and conceptual relationships between ideas and events within a passage. Examples of these words and phrases include coordinate conjunctions (e.g., and, but, yet), subordinate conjunctions (e.g., because, although, since, after), and other connective words and phrases (e,g, too, also, on the other hand, as a result).

Listed below are types of logical relationships expressed by conjunctive, or connective words. Also listed are examples of words used to cue relationships to the reader.

Additive and comparative words and phrases: and, in addition to, too, also, furthermore, similarly

Adversative and contrastive words and phrases: yet, though, only, but, however, instead, rather, on the other hand, in contrast, conversely

Causal words or phrases: so, therefore, because, as a result, if...then, unless, except, in that case, under the circumstances

Temporal words and phrases: before, after, when, while, initially, lastly, finally, until.

Examples

1.   I enjoy fast-paced sports like tennis and volleyball, but my brother prefers _____ sports.

A. running   B. slower
C. team   D. active

Q. What is the connective word that tells you to look for a contrast relationship between the two clauses?
A   The connective word *but* signals that a contrast relationship exists between the two parts of the sentence.

Q. Of the four options, what is the best choice for the blank?
A   The word *slower* is the best response here.

2.   The child stepped to close to the edge of the brook. As a result, he _____ in.

A. fell   B. waded
C. ran   D. jumped

Q. What is the connective phrase that links the two sentences?
A. The connective phrase *as a result* links the two sentences.

Q. Of the four relationships of words and phrases listed previously, what kind of relationship between the two sentences does the connective phrase in the example signal to the reader?
A. The phrase *as a result* signals that a cause and effect relationship exists between the two sentences.

Q. Identify the correct response which makes the second sentence reflect the cause and effect relationship.
A. The correct response is *fell*.

Understanding connectives is very important to success on the examination reading sub-test. Sentences with deletions are often very closely related to adjacent sentences in meaning, and the relationship is often signaled by connective words or phrases. Here is an example from the practice passage about universities.

> At first, these tutors had not been associated with one another. Rather, they had been _____. But, over time, they joined together to form guilds.

    A. curious   B. poor
    C. religious   D. ready
    E. independent

Q. Identify the connective and contrastive words and phrases in the example.

A. *At first* and *over time* are connective phrases that set up temporal progression. *Rather* and *but* are contrastive items. The use of *rather* in the sentence with the deletion tells the reader that the missing word has to convey a meaning in contrast to *associated with one another*. (Notice also that *rather* occurs after a negative statement.) The use of *but* in the sentence after the one with the deletion indicates that the deleted word in the previous sentence has to reflect a meaning that contrasts with *joined together*. Thus, the reader is given two substantial cues to the meaning of the missing word. *Independent* is the only choice that meets the requirement for contrastive meaning.

10

SAMPLE QUESTIONS

DIRECTIONS: There are two passages on the following pages. In each passage some words are missing. Wherever a word is missing, there is a blank line with a number on it. Below the passage you will find the same number and five words. Choose the word that makes the best sense in the blank. You may not be sure of the answer to a question until you read the sentences that come after the blank, so be sure to read enough to answer the questions. As you work on these passages, you will find that the second passage is harder to read than the first. Answer as many questions as you can.

Bridges are built to allow a continuous flow of highway and railway traffic across water lying in their paths. But engineers cannot forget that river traffic, too, is essential to our economy. The role of ____1____ is important. To keep these vessels moving freely, bridges are built high enough, when possible, to let them pass underneath. Sometimes, however, channels must accommodate very tall ships. It may be uneconomical to build a tall enough bridge. The ____2____ would be too high. To save money, engineers build movable bridges.

In the swing bridge, the middle part pivots or swings open. When the bridge is closed, this section joins the two ends of the bridge, blocking tall vessels. But this section ____3____. When swung open, it is perpendicular to the ends of the bridge, creating two free channels for river traffic. With swing bridges channel width is limited by the bridge's piers. The largest swing bridge provides only a 75-meter channel. Such channels are sometimes too ____4____. In such cases, a bascule bridge may be built.

Bascule bridges are drawbridges with two arms that swing upward. They provide an opening as wide as the span. They are also versatile. These bridges are not limited to being fully opened or fully closed. They can be ____5____ in many ways. They can be fixed at different angles to accommodate different vessels.

In vertical lift bridges, the center remains horizontal. Towers at both ends allow the center to be lifted like an elevator. One interesting variation of this kind of bridge was built during World War II. A lift bridge was desired, but there were wartime shortages of the steel and machinery needed for the towers. It was hard to find enough ____6____. An ingenious engineer designed the bridge so that it did not have to be raised above traffic. Instead it was ____7____. It could be submerged seven meters below the surface of the river. Ships sailed over it.

1. A. wind   B. boats   C. experience
    D. wires   E. experience

2. A. levels   B. cost   C. standards
    D. waves   E. deck

3. A. stands   B. floods   C. wears
    D. turns   E. supports

4. A. narrow   B. rough   C. long
    D. deep   E. straight

5. A. crossed   B. approached   C. lighted
    D. planned   E. positioned

6. A. work   B. material   C. time
    D. power   E. space

7. A. burned   B. emptied   C. secured
    D. shared   E. lowered

The first universities emerged at the end of the 11th century and beginning of the 12th. These institutions were not founded on any particular date or created by any formal action.

Nobody actually ____8____ them. Instead, they developed gradually in places like Paris, Oxford, and Bologna, where scholars had long been teaching students. At first, these tutors

had not been associated with one another. Rather, they had been ____9____ . But, over time, they joined together to form guilds.

Guilds were groups of tradespeople, somewhat akin to modern unions. In the Middle

Ages, all the crafts had such ____10____ . The scholars' guilds built school buildings and evolved an administration which charged fees and set standards for the curriculum. It set prices for members' services and fixed requirements for entering the profession.

Professors were not the only schoolpeople forming associations. In Italy, students joined guilds to which teachers had to swear obedience. The students set strict rules, fining professors for beginning class a minute late. Teachers had to seek their students' permission to

marry, and such permission was not always granted. Sometimes the students ____11____ . Even if they said yes, the teacher got only one day's honeymoon.

Undergraduates took classes in Greek philosophy, Latin grammar, arithmetic, music, and

astronomy. These were the only ____12____ available. More advanced study was possible in law, medicine, and theology, but one could not earn such postgraduate degrees quickly. It

took a long time to ____13____ . Completing the requirements in theology, for example, took at least 13 years.

The concept of a fixed program of study leading to a degree first evolved in medieval

Europe. This ____14____ had not appeared before. In earlier academic settings, notions about *meeting requirements* and *graduating* had been absent. Since the Middle Ages, though, we have continued to view education as a set curriculum culminating in a degree.

8.   A. started   B. guarded   C. blamed
     D. compared   E. remembered

9.   A. curious   B. poor   C. religious
     D. curious   E. independent

10. A. taxes   B. secrets   C. products
     D. problems   E. organizations

11. A. left   B. copied   C. refused
     D. paid   E. prepared

12. A. rooms   B. subjects   C. clothes
     D. pens   E. markets

13. A. add   B. answer   C. forget
     D. finish   E. travel

14. A. idea   B. desk   C. library
     D. capital   E. company

———

KEY (CORRECT ANSWERS)

1.	B		6.	B	
2.	B		7.	E	
3.	D		8.	A	
4.	A		9.	E	
5.	E		10.	E	

11.	C
12.	B
13.	D
14.	A

———

READING COMPREHENSION
UNDERSTANDING AND INTERPRETING WRITTEN MATERIAL
COMMENTARY

The ability to read and understand written materials – texts, publications, newspapers, orders, directions, expositions – is a skill basic to a functioning democracy and to an efficient business or viable government.

That is why almost all examinations – for beginning, middle, and senior levels – test reading comprehension, directly or indirectly.

The reading test measures how well you understand what you read. This is how it is done: You read a short paragraph and five statements. From the five statements, you choose the one statement, or answer, that is BEST supported by, or best matches, what is said in the paragraph.

SAMPLE QUESTIONS

DIRECTIONS: Each question has five suggested answers, lettered A, B, C, D, and E. Decide which one is the BEST answer. *PRINT THE LETTER OF THE CORRECT ANSWER IN THE SPACE AT THE RIGHT.*

1.   The prevention of accidents makes it necessary not only that safety devices be used to guard exposed machinery but also that mechanics be instructed in safety rules which they must follow for their own protection and that the light in the plant be adequate. The paragraph BEST supports the statement that industrial accidents

    1.____

    A.   are always avoidable
    B.   may be due to ignorance
    C.   usually result from inadequate machinery
    D.   cannot be entirely overcome
    E.   result in damage to machinery

ANALYSIS

Remember what you have to do–
    First   - Read the paragraph.
    Second - Decide what the paragraph means.
    Third   - Read the five suggested answers.
    Fourth   - Select the one answer which BEST matches what the paragraph says or is BEST supported by something in the paragraph. (Sometimes you may have to read the paragraph again in order to be sure which suggested answer is best.)

This paragraph is talking about three steps that should be taken to prevent industrial accidents–

    1.   use safety devices on machines
    2.   instruct mechanics in safety rules
    3.   provide adequate lighting.

SELECTION

With this in mind let's look at each suggested answer. Each one starts with "Industrial accidents..."

SUGGESTED ANSWER A.
Industrial accidents (A) are always avoidable.
(The paragraph talks about how to avoid accidents, but does not say that accidents are always avoidable.)

SUGGESTED ANSWER B.
Industrial accidents (b) may be due to ignorance.
(One of the steps given in the paragraph to prevent accidents is to instruct mechanics on safety rules. This suggests that lack of knowledge or ignorance of safety rules causes accidents. This suggested answer sounds like a good possibility for being the right answer.)

SUGGESTED ANSWER C.
Industrial accidents (C) usually result from inadequate machinery.
(The paragraph does suggest that exposed machines cause accidents, but it doesn't say that it is the usual cause of accidents. The word usually makes this a wrong answer.)

SUGGESTED ANSWER D.
Industrial accidents (D) cannot be entirely overcome.
(You may know from your own experience that this is a true statement. But that is not what the paragraph is talking about. Therefore it is NOT the correct answer.)

SUGGESTED ANSWER E.
Industrial accidents (E) result in damage to machinery.
(This is a statement that may or may not be true, but in any case it is NOT covered by the paragraph.)

_____

Looking back, you see that the one suggested answer of the five given that BEST matches what the paragraph says is—
Industrial accidents (B) may be due to ignorance.
The CORRECT answer then is B.

Be sure you read ALL the possible answers before you make your choice. You may think that none of the five answers is really good, but choose the BEST one of the five.

_____

2. Probably few people realize, as they drive on a concrete road, that steel is used to keep   2.____
the surface flat in spite of the weight of the busses and trucks. Steel bars, deeply embedded in the concrete, provide sinews to take the stresses so that the stresses cannot
crack the slab or make it wavy.
The paragraph BEST supports the statement that a concrete road

    A.   is expensive to build
    B.   usually cracks under heavy weights
    C.   looks like any other road
    D.   is used only for heavy traffic
    E.   is reinforced with other material

ANALYSIS

This paragraph is commenting on the fact that–
    1.   few people realize, as they drive on a concrete road, that steel is deeply
         embedded
    2.   steel keeps the surface flat
    3.   steel bars enable the road to take the stresses without cracking or becom-
         ing wavy.

SELECTION

Now read and think about the possible answers:
    A.   A concrete road is expensive to build. (Maybe so but that is not what the paragraph
         is about.)
    B.   A concrete road usually cracks under heavy weights. (The paragraph talks about
         using steel bars to prevent heavy weights from cracking concrete roads. It says
         nothing about how usual it is for the roads to crack. The word usually makes this
         suggested answer wrong.)
    C.   A concrete road looks like any other road. (This may or may not be true. The impor-
         tant thing to note is that it has nothing to do with what the paragraph is about.)
    D.   A concrete road is used only for heavy traffic. (This answer at least has something
         to do with the paragraph-concrete roads are used with heavy traffic but it does not
         say "used only.")
    E.   A concrete road is reinforced with other material. (This choice seems to be the cor-
         rect one on two counts: First, the paragraph does suggest that concrete roads are
         made stronger by embedding steel bars in them. This is another way of saying
         "concrete roads are reinforced with steel bars." Second, by the process of elimina-
         tion, the other four choices are ruled out as correct answers simply because they
         do not apply.)

You can be sure that not all the reading questions will be so easy as these.

———————

HINTS FOR ANSWERING READING QUESTIONS

1. Read the paragraph carefully. Then read each suggested answer carefully. Read every word, because often one word can make the difference between a right and a wrong answer.

2. Choose that answer which is supported in the paragraph itself. Do not choose an answer which is a correct statement unless it is based on information in the paragraph.

3. Even though a suggested answer has many of the words used in the paragraph, it may still be wrong.

4. Look out for words – such as *always, never, entirely, or only* – which tend to make a suggested answer wrong.

5. Answer first those questions which you can answer most easily. Then work on the other questions.

6. If you can't figure out the answer to the question, guess.

———

READING COMPREHENSION
UNDERSTANDING AND INTERPRETING WRITTEN MATERIAL
EXAMINATION SECTION
TEST 1

DIRECTIONS: Each question has five suggested answers, lettered A to E. Decide which one
is the BEST answer. *PRINT THE LETTER OF THE CORRECT ANSWER IN
THE SPACE AT THE RIGHT.*

1.   Some specialists are willing to give their services to the Government entirely free of   1._____
charge; some feel that a nominal salary, such as will cover traveling expenses, is sufficient for a position that is recognized as being somewhat honorary in nature; many other
specialists value their time so highly that they will not devote any of it to public service
that does not repay them at a rate commensurate with the fees that they can obtain from
a good private clientele.
*The paragraph BEST supports the statement that the use of specialists by the Govern-
ment*

   A.   is rare because of the high cost of securing such persons
   B.   may be influenced by the willingness of specialists to serve
   C.   enables them to secure higher salaries in private fields
   D.   has become increasingly common during the past few years
   E.   always conflicts with private demands for their services

2.   The fact must not be overlooked that only about one-half of the international trade of the   2._____
world crosses the oceans. The other half is merely exchanges of merchandise between
countries lying alongside each other or at least within the same continent.
The paragraph BEST supports the statement that

   A.   the most important part of any country's trade is transoceanic
   B.   domestic trade is insignificant when compared with foreign trade
   C.   the exchange of goods between neighborhing countries is not considerd interna-
tional trade
   D.   foreign commerce is not necessarily carried on by water
   E.   about one-half of the trade of the world is international

3.   Individual differences in mental traits assume importance in fitting workers to jobs   3._____
because such personal characteristics are persistent and are relatively little influenced
by training and experience.
The paragraph BEST supports the statement that training and experience

   A.   are limited in their effectiveness in fitting workers to jobs
   B.   do not increase a worker's fitness for a job
   C.   have no effect upon a person's mental traits
   D.   have relatively little effect upon the individual's chances for success
   E.   should be based on the mental traits of an individual

4. The competition of buyers tends to keep prices up, the competition of sellers to send   4.___
    them down. Normally the pressure of competition among sellers is stronger than that
    among buyers since the seller has his article to sell and must get rid of it, whereas the
    buyer is not committed to anything.
    The paragraph BEST supports the statement that low prices are caused by

    A. buyer competition
    B. competition of buyers with sellers
    C. fluctuations in demand
    D. greater competition among sellers than among buyers
    E. more sellers than buyers

5. In seventeen states, every lawyer is automatically a member of the American Bar Associ-   5.___
    ation. In some other states and localities, truly representative organizations of the Bar
    have not yet come into being, but are greatly needed.
    The paragraph IMPLIES that

    A. representative Bar Associations are necessary in states where they do not now
        exist
    B. every lawyer is required by law to become a member of the Bar
    C. the Bar Association is a democratic organization
    D. some states have more lawyers than others
    E. every member of the American Bar Association is automatically a lawyer in seven-
        teen states.

KEY (CORRECT ANSWERS)

1. B
2. D
3. A
4. D
5. A

TEST 2

DIRECTIONS: Each question has five suggested answers, lettered A to E. Decide which one is the BEST answer. *PRINT THE LETTER OF THE CORRECT ANSWER IN THE SPACE AT THE RIGHT.*

1. We hear a great deal about the new education, and see a great deal of it in action. But the school house, though prodigiously magnified in scale, is still very much the same old school house.
   The paragraph IMPLIES that

   A. the old education was, after all, better than the new
   B. although the modern school buildings are larger than the old ones, they have not changed very much in other respects
   C. the old school houses do not fit in with modern educational theories
   D. a fine school building does not make up for poor teachers
   E. schools will be schools

   1.____

2. No two human beings are of the same pattern — not even twins and the method of bringing out the best in each one necessarily varies according to the nature of the child.
   The paragraph IMPLIES that

   A. individual differences should be considered in dealing with children
   B. twins should be treated impartially
   C. it is an easy matter to determine the special abilities of children
   D. a child's nature varies from year to year
   E. we must discover the general technique of dealing with children

   2.____

3. Man inhabits today a world very different from that which encompassed even his parents and grandparents. It is a world geared to modern machinery—automobiles, airplanes, power plants; it is linked together and served by electricity.
   The paragraph IMPLIES that

   A. the world has not changed much during the last few generations
   B. modern inventions and discoveries have brought about many changes in man's way of living
   C. the world is run more efficiently today than it was in our grandparents' time
   D. man is much happier today than he was a hundred years ago
   E. we must learn to see man as he truly is, underneath the veneers of man's contrivances

   3.____

4. Success in any study depends largely upon the interest taken in that particular subject by the student. This being the case, each teacher earnestly hopes that her students will realize at the very outset that shorthand can be made an intensely fascinating study.
   The paragraph IMPLIES that

   A. everyone is interested in shorthand
   B. success in a study is entirely impossible unless the student finds the study very interesting
   C. if a student is eager to study shorthand, he is likely to succeed in it
   D. shorthand is necessary for success
   E. anyone who is not interested in shorthand will not succeed in business

   4.____

5. The primary purpose of all business English is to move the reader to agreeable and   5.___
    mutually profitable action. This action may be indirect or direct, but in either case a highly
    competitive appeal for business should be clothed with incisive diction tending to replace
    vagueness and doubt with clarity, confidence, and appropriate action.
    The paragraph IMPLIES that the

    A.   ideal business letter uses words to conform to the reader's language level
    B.   business correspondent should strive for conciseness in letter writing
    C.   keen competition of today has lessened the value of the letter as an appeal for business
    D.   writer of a business letter should employ incisive diction to move the reader to compliant and gainful action
    E.   the writer of a business letter should be himself clear, confident, and Forceful

---

KEY (CORRECT ANSWERS)

1. B
2. A
3. B
4. C
5. D

TEST 3

DIRECTIONS: Each question has five suggested answers, lettered A to E. Decide which one is the BEST answer. *PRINT THE LETTER OF THE CORRECT ANSWER IN THE SPACE AT THE RIGHT.*

1. To serve the community best, a comprehensive city plan must coordinate all physical improvements, even at the possible expense of subordinating individual desires, to the end that a city may grow in a more orderly way and provide adequate facilities for its people.
   The paragraph IMPLIES that

   A. city planning provides adequate facilities for recreation
   B. a comprehensive city plan provides the means for a city to grow in a more orderly fashion
   C. individual desires must always be subordinated to civic changes
   D. the only way to serve a community is to adopt a comprehensive city plan
   E. city planning is the most important function of city government

1.____

2. Facility in writing letters, the knack of putting into these quickly written letters the same personal impression that would mark an interview, and the ability to boil down to a one-page letter the gist of what might be called a five- or ten-minute conversation—all these are essential to effective work under conditions of modern business organization.
   The paragraph IMPLIES that

   A. letters are of more importance in modern business activities than ever before
   B. letters should be used in place of interviews
   C. the ability to write good letters is essential to effective work in modern business organization
   D. business letters should never be more than one page in length
   E. the person who can write a letter with great skill will get ahead more readily than others

2.____

3. The general rule is that it is the city council which determines the amount to be raised by taxation and which therefore determines, within the law, the tax rates. As has been pointed out, however, no city council or city authority has the power to determine what kinds of taxes should be levied.
   The paragraph IMPLIES that

   A. the city council has more authority than any other municipal body
   B. while the city council has a great deal of authority in the levying of taxes, its power is not absolute
   C. the kinds of taxes levied in different cities vary greatly
   D. the city council appoints the tax collectors
   E. the mayor determines the kinds of taxes to be levied

3.____

4. The growth of modern business has made necessary mass production, mass distribution, and mass selling. As a result, the problems of personnel and industrial relations have increased so rapidly that grave injustices in the handling of personal relationships have frequently occurred. Personnel administration is complex because, as in all human problems, many intangible elements are involved. Therefore a thorough, systematic, and continuous study of the psychology of human behavior is essential to the intelligent handling of personnel.
   The paragraph IMPLIES that

4.____

A. complex modern industry makes impossible the personal relationships which formerly existed between employer and employee
B. mass decisions are successfully applied to personnel problems
C. the human element in personnel administration makes continuous study necessary to its intelligent application
D. personnel problems are less important than the problems of mass production and mass distribution
E. since personnel administration is so complex and costly, it should be sub-ordinated to the needs of good industrial relations

5. The Social Security Act is striving toward the attainment of economic security for the individual and for his family. It was stated, in outlining this program, that security for the individual and for the family concerns itself with three factors: (1) decent homes to live in; (2) development of the natural resources of the country so as to afford the fullest opportunity to engage in productive work; and (3) safeguards against the major misfortunes of life. The Social Security Act is concerned with the third of these factors – "safeguards against misfortunes which cannot be wholly eliminated in this man-made world of ours."
   The paragraph IMPLIES that the

5.___

A. Social Security Act is concerned primarily with supplying to families decent homes in which to live
B. development of natural resources is the only means of offering employment to the
C. masses of the unemployed
   Social Security Act has attained absolute economic security for the individual and his family
D. Social Security Act deals with the first (1) factor as stated in the paragraph above
E. Social Security Act deals with the third (3) factor as stated in the paragraph above

———

KEY (CORRECT ANSWERS)

1. B
2. C
3. B
4. C
5. E

———

38

TEST 4

PASSAGE 1

Free unrhymed verse has been practiced for some thousands of years and reaches back to the incantation which linked verse with the ritual dance. It provided a communal emotion; the aim of the cadenced phrases was to create a state of mind. The general coloring of free rhythms in the poetry of today is that of speech rhythm, composed in the sequence of the musical phrase, not in the sequence of the metronome, the regular beat. In the twenties, conventional rhyme fell into almost complete disuse. This liberation from rhyme became as well a liberation of rhyme. Freed of its exacting task of supporting lame verse, it would be applied with greater effect where wanted for some special effect. Such break in the tradition of rhymed verse had the healthy effect of giving it a fresh start, released from the hampering convention of too familiar cadences. This refreshing and subtilizing of the use of rhyme can be seen everywhere in the poetry today.

1. The title below that BEST expresses the ideas of this paragraph is: 1.____

    A. Primitive Poetry
    B. The Origin of Poetry
    C. Rhyme and Rhythm in Modern Verse
    D. Classification of Poetry
    E. Purposes in All Poetry

2. Free verse had its origin in primitive   2.____

    A. fairytales   B. literature   C. warfare
    D. chants   E. courtship

3. The object of early free verse was to   3.____

    A. influence the mood of the people   B. convey ideas
    C. produce mental pictures   D. create pleasing sounds
    E. provide enjoyment

PASSAGE 2

Control of the Mississippi had always been goals of nations having ambitions in the New World. La Salle claimed it for France in 1682. Iberville appropriated it to France when he colonized Louisiana in 1700. Bienville founded New Orleans, its principal port, as a French city in 1718. The fleur-de-lis were the blazon of the delta country until 1762. Then Spain claimed all of Louisiana. The Spanish were easy neighbors. American products from western Pennsylvania and the North west Territory were barged down the Ohio and Mississippi to New Orleans, here they were reloaded on ocean-going vessels that cleared for the great seaports of the world.

1. The title below that BEST expresses the ideas of this paragraph is: 1.____

    A. Importance of seaports
    B. France and Spain in the New World
    C. Early control of the Mississippi
    D. Claims of European nations
    E. American trade on the Mississippi

2. Until 1762 the lower Mississippi area was held by   2.__

   A. England   B. Spain   C. the United States
   D. France   E. Indians

3. In doing business with Americans the Spaniards were   3.__

   A. easy to outsmart
   B. friendly to trade
   C. inclined to charge high prices for use of their ports
   D. shrewd
   E. suspicious

PASSAGE 3

Our humanity is by no means so materialistic as foolish talk is continually asserting it to be. Judging by what I have learned about men and women, I am convinced that there is far more in them of idealistic willpower than ever comes to the surface of the world. Just as the water of streams is small in amount compared to that which flows underground, so the idealism which becomes visible is small in amount compared with that which men and women bear locked in their hearts, unreleased or scarcely released. To unbind what is bound, to bring the underground waters to the surface — mankind is waiting and longing for men who can do that.

1. The title below that BEST expresses the ideas of this paragraph is   1._

   A. Releasing Underground Riches
   B. The Good and Bad in Man
   C. Materialism in Humanity
   D. The Surface and the Depths of Idealism
   E. Unreleased Energy

2. Human beings are more idealistic than   2._

   A. the water in underground streams
   B. their waiting and longing proves
   C. outward evidence shows
   D. the world
   E. other living creatures

PASSAGE 4

The total impression made by any work of fiction cannot be rightly understood without a sympathetic perception of the artistic aims of the writer. Consciously or unconsciouly, he has accepted certain facts, and rejected or suppressed other facts, in order to give unity to the particular aspect of human life which he is depicting. No novelist possesses the impartiality, the indifference, the infinite tolerance of nature. Nature displays to use, with complete unconcern, the beautiful and the ugly, the precious and the trivial, the pure and the impure. But a writer must select the aspects of nature and human nature which are demanded by the work in hand. He is forced to select, to combine, to create.

1. The title below that BEST expresses the ideas of this paragraph is: 1.____

    A.   Impressionists in Literature
    B.   Nature as an Artist
    C.   The Novelist as an Imitator
    D.   Creative Technic of the Novelist
    E.   Aspects of Nature

2. A novelist rejects some facts because they   2.____

    A.   are impure and ugly
    B.   would show he is not impartial
    C.   are unrelated to human nature
    D.   would make a bad impression
    E.   mar the unity of his story

3. It is important for a reader to know   3.____

    A.   the purpose of the author
    B.   what facts the author omits
    C.   both the ugly and the beautiful
    D.   something about nature
    E.   what the author thinks of human nature

PASSAGE 5

If you watch a lamp which is turned very rapidly on and off, and you keep your eyes open, "persistence of vision" will bridge the gaps of darkness between the flashes of light, and the lamp will seem to be continuously lit. This "topical afterglow" explains the magic produced by the stroboscope, a new instrument which seems to freeze the swiftest motions while they are still going on, and to stop time itself dead in its tracks. The "magic" is all in the eye of the beholder.

1. The "magic" of the stroboscope is due to   1.____

    A.   continuous lighting   B.   intense cold
    C.   slow motion   D.   behavior of the human eye
    E.   a lapse of time

2. "Persistence of vision" is explained by   2.____

    A.   darkness   B.   winking   C.   rapid flashes
    D.   gaps   E.   after impression

KEY (CORRECT ANSWERS)

PASSAGE 1

1. C
2. D
3. A

PASSAGE 2

1. C
2. D
3. B

PASSAGE 3

1. D
2. C

PASSAGE 4

1. D
2. E
3. A

PASSAGE 5

1. D
2. E

TEST 5

PASSAGE 1

During the past fourteen years, thousands of top-lofty United States elms have been marked for death by the activities of the tiny European elm bark beetle. The beetles, however, do not do fatal damage. Death is caused by another importation, Dutch elm disease, a fungus infection which the beetles carry from tree to tree. Up to 1941, quarantine and tree-sanitation measures kept the beetles and the disease pretty well confined within 510 miles around metropolitan New York. War curtailed these measures and made Dutch elm disease a wider menace. Every house hold and village that prizes an elm-shaded lawn or commons must now watch for it. Since there is as yet no cure for it, the infected trees must be pruned or felled, and the wood must be burned in order to protect other healthy trees.

1. The title below that BEST expresses the ideas of this paragraph is: 1.____

   A. A Menace to Our Elms
   C. Our Vanishing Elms
   E. How Elms are Protected
   B. Pests and Diseases of the Elm
   D. The Need to Protect Dutch Elms

2. The danger of spreading the Dutch elm disease was increased by 2.____

   A. destroying infected trees
   C. the lack of a cure
   E. quarantine measures
   B. the war
   D. a fungus infection

3. The European elm bark beetle is a serious threat to our elms because it 3.____

   A. chews the bark
   B. kills the trees
   C. is particularly active on the eastern seaboard
   D. carries infection
   E. cannot be controlled

PASSAGE 2

It is elemental that the greater the development of man, the greater the problems he has to concern him. When he lived in a cave with stone implements, his mind no less than his actions was grooved into simple channels. Every new invention, every new way of doing things posed fresh problems for him. And, as he moved along the road, he questioned each step, as indeed he should, for he trod upon the beliefs of his ancestors. It is equally elemental to say that each step upon this later road posed more questions than the earlier ones. It is only the edcated man who realizes the results of his actions; it is only the thoughtful one who questions his own decisions.

1. The title below that BEST expresses the ideas of this paragraph is: 1.____

   A. Channels of Civilization
   B. The Mark of a Thoughtful Man
   C. The Cave Man in Contrast with Man Today
   D. The Price of Early Progress
   E. Man's Never-Ending Challenge

PASSAGE 3

Spring is one of those things that man has no hand in, any more than he has a part in sunrise or the phases of the moon. Spring came before man was here to enjoy it, and it will go right on coming even if man isn't here some time in the future. It is a matter of solar mechanics and celestial order. And for all our knowledge of astronomy and terrestrial mechanics, we haven't yet been able to do more than bounce a radar beam off the moon. We couldn't alter the arrival of the spring equinox by as much as one second, if we tried.

Spring is a matter of growth, of chlorophyll, of bud and blossom. We can alter growth and change the time of blossoming in individual plants; but the forests still grow in nature's way, and the grass of the plains hasn't altered its nature in a thousand years. Spring is a magnificent phase of the cycle of nature; but man really hasn't any guiding or controlling hand in it. He is here to enjoy it and benefit by it. And April is a good time to realize it; by May perhaps we will want to take full credit.

1. The title below that BEST expresses the ideas of this passage is: 1._

    A. The Marvels of the Spring Equinox
    B. Nature's Dependence on Mankind
    C. The Weakness of Man Opposed to Nature
    D. The Glories of the World
    E. Eternal Growth

2. The author of the passage states that 2._

    A. man has a part in the phases of the moon
    B. April is a time for taking full-credit
    C. April is a good time to enjoy nature
    D. man has a guiding hand in spring
    E. spring will cease to be if civilization ends

PASSAGE 4

The walled medieval town was as characteristic of its period as the cut of a robber baron's beard. It sprang out of the exigencies of war, and it was not without its architectural charm, whatever its hygienic deficiencies may have been. Behind its high, thick walls not only the normal inhabitants but the whole countryside fought and cowered in an hour of need. The capitals of Europe now forsake the city when the sirens scream and death from the sky seems imminent. Will the fear of bombs accelerate the slow decentralization which began with the automobile and the wide distribution of electrical energy and thus reverse the medieval flow to the city?

1. The title below that BEST expresses the ideas in this paragraph is.

    A. A Changing Function of the Town   B. The Walled Medieval Town
    C. The Automobile's Influence on City   D. Forsaking the City
        Life
    E. Bombs Today and Yesterday

2. Conditions in the Middle Ages made the walled town

    A. a natural development   B. the most dangerous of all places
    C. a victim of fires   D. lacking in architectural charm
    E. healthful

3.   Modern conditions may   3._____

    A.   make cities larger   B.   make cities more hygienic
    C.   protect against floods   D.   cause people to move from population
    E.   encourage good architecture   centers

PASSAGE 5

The literary history of this nation began when the first settler from abroad of sensitive mind paused in his adventure long enough to feel that he was under a different sky, breathing new air, and that a New World was all before him with only his strength and Providence for guides. With him began a new emphasis upon an old theme in literature, the theme of cutting loose and faring forth, renewed, under the powerful influence of a fresh continent for civilized man. It has provided, ever since those first days, a strong current in our native literature, whose other flow has come from a nostalgia for the rich culture of Europe, so much of which was perforce left behind.

1.   The title below that BEST expresses the ideas of this paragraph is: 1._____

    A.   America's Distinctive Literature   B.   Pioneer Authors
    C.   The Dead Hand of the Past   D.   Europe's Literary Grandchild
    E.   America Comes of Age

2.   American writers, according to the author, because of their colonial experiences   2._____

    A.   were antagonistic to European writers
    B.   cut loose from Old World influences
    C.   wrote only on New World events and characters
    D.   created new literary themes
    E.   gave fresh interpretation to an old literary idea

KEY (CORRECT ANSWERS)

PASSAGE 1	PASSAGE 2
1. A	1. E
2. B	
3. D	

PASSAGE 3	PASSAGE 4
1. C	1. A
2. C	2. A
	3. D

PASSAGE 5

1. A
2. E

TEST 6

1. Any business not provided with capable substitutes to fill all important positions is a weak business. Therefore a foreman should train each man not only to perform his own particular duties but also to do those of two or three positions.
    The paragraph BEST supports the statement that

    A. dependence on substitutes is a sign of weak organization
    B. training will improve the strongest organization
    C. the foreman should be the most expert at any particular job under him
    D. every employee can be trained to perform efficiently work other than his own
    E. vacancies in vital positions should be provided for in advance

2. The coloration of textile fabrics composed of cotton and wool generally requires two processes, as the process used in dyeing wool is seldom capable of fixing the color upon cotton. The usual method is to immerse the fabric in the requisite baths to dye the wool and then to treat the partially dyed material in the manner found suitable for cotton.
    The paragraph BEST supports the statement that the dyeing of textile fabrics composed of cotton and wool

    A. is less complicated than the dyeing of wool alone
    B. is more successful when the material contains more cotton than wool
    C. is not satisfactory when solid colors are desired
    D. is restricted to two colors for any one fabric
    E. is usually based upon the methods required for dyeing the different materials

3. The serious investigator must direct his whole effort toward. success in his work. If he wishes to succeed in each investigation, his work will be by no means easy, smooth, or peaceful; on the contrary, he will have to devote himself completely and continuously to a task that requires all his ability.
    The paragraph BEST supports the statement that an investigator's success depends most upon

    A. ambition to advance rapidly in the service
    B. persistence in the face of difficulty
    C. training and experience
    D. willingness to obey orders without delay
    E. the number of investigations which he conducts

4. Honest people in one nation find it difficult to understand the viewpoint of honest people in another. State departments and their ministers exist for the purpose of explaining the viewpoints of one nation in terms understood by another. Some of their most important work lies in this direction.
    The paragraph BEST supports the statement that

    A. people of different nations may not consider matters in the same light
    B. it is unusual for many people to share similar ideas
    C. suspicion prevents understanding between nations
    D. the chief work of state departments is to guide relations between nations united by a common cause
    E. the people of one nation must sympathize with the view points of others

5. Economy once in a while is just not enough. I expect to find it at every level of responsi-   5._____
    bility, from cabinet member to the newest and youngest recruit. Controlling waste is
    something like bailing a boat; you have to keep at it. I have no intention of easing up on
    my insistence on getting a dollar of value for each dollar we spend.
    The paragraph BEST supports the statement that

    A. we need not be concerned about items which cost less than a dollar
    B. it is advisable to buy the cheaper of two items
    C. the responsibility of economy is greater at high levels than at low levels
    D. economy becomes easy with practice
    E. economy is a continuing responsibility

___

KEY (CORRECT ANSWERS)

1. E
2. E
3. B
4. A
5. E

___

TEST 7

1. On all permit imprint mail the charge for postage has been printed by the mailer before   1.___
he presents it for mailing and pays the postage. Such mail of any class is mailable only at
the post office that issued a permit covering it. Since the postage receipts for such mail
represent only the amount of permit imprint mail detected and verified, employees in
receiving, handling, and outgoing sections must be alert constantly to route such mail to
the weighing section before it is handled or dispatched.
The paragraph BEST supports the statement that, at post offices where permit mail is
received for dispatch,

    A. dispatching units make a final check on the amount of postage payable on permit
       imprint mail
    B. employees are to check the postage chargeable on mail received under permit
    C. neither more nor less postage is to be collected than the amount printed on permit
       imprint mail
    D. the weighing section is primarily responsible for failure to collect postage on such
       mail
    E. unusual measures are taken to prevent unstamped mail from being accepted

2. Education should not stop when the individual has been prepared to make a livelihood   2.___
and to live in modern society. Living would be mere existence were there no appreciation
and enjoyment of the riches of art, literature, and science.
The paragraph BEST supports the statement that true education

    A. is focused on the routine problems of life
    B. prepares one for full enjoyment of life
    C. deals chiefly with art, literature and science
    D. is not possible for one who does not enjoy scientific literature
    E. disregards practical ends

3. Insured and c.o.d. air and surface mail is accepted with the understanding that the   3.___
sender guarantees any necessary forwarding or return postage. When such mail is forwarded or returned, it shall be rated up for collection of postage; except that insured or
c.o.d. air mail weighing 8 ounces or less and subject to the 40 cents an ounce rate shall
be forwarded by air if delivery will be advanced, and returned by surface means, without
additional postage.
The paragraph BEST supports the statement that the return postage for undeliverable
insured mail is

    A. included in the original prepayment on air mail parcels
    B. computed but not collected before dispatching surface patrol post mail to sender
    C. not computed or charged for any air mail that is returned by surface transportation
    D. included in the amount collected when the sender mails parcel post
    E. collected before dispatching for return if any amount due has been guaranteed

4. All undeliverable first-class mail, except first-class parcels and parcel post paid with first-   4.___
class postage, which cannot be returned to the sender, is sent to a dead-letter branch.
Undeliverable matter of the third-and fourth-classes of obvious value for which the
sender does not furnish return postage and undeliverable first-class parcels and parcel-
post matter bearing postage of the first-class, which cannot be returned, is sent to a
dead parcel-post branch.

The paragraph BEST supports the statement that matter that is sent to a dead parcel-post branch includes all undeliverable

A. mail, except first-class letter mail, that appears to be valuable
B. mail, except that of the first-class, on which the sender failed to prepay the original mailing costs
C. parcels on which the mailer prepaid the first-class rate of postage
D. third-and fourth-class matter on which the required return postage has not been paid
E. parcels on which first-class postage has been prepaid, when the sender's address is not known

5. Civilization started to move rapidly when man freed himself of the shackles that restricted his search for truth.
   The paragraph BEST supports the statement that the progress of civilization   5.____

A. came as a result of man's dislike for obstacles
B. did not begin until restrictions on learning were removed
C. has been aided by man's efforts to find the truth
D. is based on continually increasing efforts
E. continues at a constantly increasing rate

KEY (CORRECT ANSWERS)

1. B
2. B
3. B
4. E
5. C

TEST 8

1. E-mails should be clear, concise, and brief. Omit all unnecessary words. The parts of speech most often used in e-mails are nouns, verbs, adjectives, and adverbs. If possible, do without pronouns, prepositions, articles, and copulative verbs. Use simple sentences, rather than complex and compound.
    The paragraph BEST supports the statement that in writing e-mails one should always use

    A. common and simple words
    B. only nouns, verbs, adjectives, and adverbs
    C. incomplete sentences
    D. only words essential to the meaning
    E. the present tense of verbs

2. The function of business is to increase the wealth of the country and the value and happiness of life. It does this by supplying the material needs of men and women. When the nation's business is successfully carried on, it renders public service of the highest value.
    The paragraph BEST supports the statement that

    A. all businesses which render public service are successful
    B. human happiness is enhanced only by the increase of material wants
    C. the value of life is increased only by the increase of wealth
    D. the material needs of men and women are supplied by welt-conducted business
    E. business is the only field of activity which increases happiness

3. In almost every community, fortunately, there are certain men and women known to be public-spirited. Others, however, may be selfish and act only as their private interests seem to require.
    The paragraph BEST supports the statement that those citizens who disregard others are

    A. fortunate   B. needed
    C. found only in small communities D. not known
    E. not public-spirited

KEY (CORRECT ANSWERS)

1. D
2. D
3. E

READING COMPREHENSION
UNDERSTANDING WRITTEN MATERIALS
COMMENTARY

The ability to read and understand written materials – texts, publications, newspapers, orders, directions, expositions – is a skill basic to a functioning democracy and to an efficient business or viable government.

That is why almost all examinations – for beginning, middle, and senior levels – test reading comprehension, directly or indirectly.

The reading test measures how well you understand what you read. This is how it is done: You read a passage followed by several statements. From these statements, you choose the *one* statement, or answer, that is BEST supported by, or BEST matches, what is said in the paragraph. *PRINT THE LETTER OF THE CORRECT ANSWER IN THE SPACE AT THE RIGHT.*

SAMPLE QUESTION

DIRECTIONS: Answer Question 1 ONLY according to the information given in the following passage :

1.   A cashier has to make many arithmetic calculations in connection with his work. Skill in   1._____
arithmetic comes readily with practice; no special talent is needed.
On the basis of the above statement, it is MOST accurate to state that

   A.   the most important part of a cashier's job is to make calculations
   B.   few cashiers have the special ability needed to handle arithmetic problems easily
   C.   without special talent, cashiers cannot learn to do the calculations they are required to do in their work
   D.   a cashier can, with practice, learn to handle the computations he is required to make.
The *correct* answer is D.

EXAMINATION SECTION
TEST 1

Questions 1-5.

DIRECTIONS: Questions 1 to 5 are based on the following reading passage:

The size of each collection route will be determined by the amount of waste per stop, distance between stops, speed of loading, speed of truck, traffic conditions during loading time, etc.

Basically, the route should consist of a proper amount of work for a crew for the daily working period. The crew should service all properties eligible for this service in their area. Routes should, whenever practical, be compact, with a logical progression through the area. Unnecessary travel should be avoided. Traffic conditions on the route should be thoroughly studied to prevent lost time in loading, to reduce hazards to employees, and to minimize tying up of regular traffic movements by collection forces. Natural and physical barriers and arterial streets should be used as route boundaries wherever possible to avoid lost time in travel.

Routes within a district should be laid out so that the crews start at the point farthest from the disposal area and, as the day progresses, move toward that area, thus reducing the length of the haul. When possible, the work of the crews in a district should be parallel as they progress throughout the day, with routes finishing up within a short distance of each other. This enables the supervisor to be present when crews are completing their work and enables him to shift crews to trouble spots to complete the day's work.

1. Based on the above passage, an **advantage** of having collection routes end near one another is that

    A. routes can be made more compact
    B. unnecessary travel is avoided, saving manpower
    C. the length of the haul is reduced
    D. the supervisor can exercise better manpower control

1.___

2. Of the factors mentioned above which affect the size of a collection route, the two over which the sanitation forces have **LEAST** control are

    A. amount of waste; traffic conditions
    B. speed of loading; amount of waste
    C. speed of truck; distance between stops
    D. traffic conditions; speed of truck

2.___

3. According to the above passage, the size of a collection route is probably good if

    A. it is a fair day's work for a normal crew
    B. it is not necessary for the trucks to travel too fast
    C. the amount of waste collected can be handled properly
    D. the distance between stops is approximately equal

3.___

4. Based on the above passage, it is reasonable to assume that a sanitation officer laying out collection routes should NOT try to have   4._____

    A.   an arterial street as a route boundary
    B.   any routes near the disposal area
    C.   the routes overlap a little
    D.   the routes run in the same direction

5. The term "logical progression" as used in the second paragraph of the passage refers MOST nearly to   5._____

    A.   collecting from street after street in order
    B.   numbering streets one after the other
    C.   rotating crew assignments
    D.   using logic as a basis for assignment of crews

———

TEST 2

Questions 1-3.

DIRECTIONS: Answer Questions 1, 2, and 3 *SOLELY* on the basis of the paragraph below.

In an open discussion designed to arrive at solutions to community problems, the person leading the discussion group should give the members a chance to make their suggestions before he makes his. He must not be afraid of silence, if he talks just to keep things going, he will find he can't stop, and good discussion will not develop. In other words, the more he talks, the more the group will depend on him. If he finds, however, that no one seems ready to begin the discussion, his best "opening" is to ask for definitions of terms which form the basis of the discussion. By pulling out as many definitions or interpretations as possible, he can get the group started "thinking out loud," which is essential to good discussion.

1. According to the above paragraph, good group discussion is *most likely* to result if the person leading the discussion group

    A. keeps the discussion going by speaking whenever the group stops speaking
    B. encourages the group to depend on him by speaking more than any other group member
    C. makes his own suggestions before the group has a chance to make theirs
    D. encourages discussion by asking the group to interpret the terms to be discussed

2. According to the paragraph above, "thinking out loud" by the discussion group is

    A. *good* practice, because "thinking out loud" is important to good discussion
    B. *poor* practice, because group members should think out their ideas before discussing them
    C. *good* practice, because it will encourage the person leading the discussion to speak more
    D. *poor* practice, because it causes the group to fear silence during a discussion

3. According to the paragraph above, the *one* of the following which is LEAST desirable at an open discussion is having

    A. silent periods during which none of the group members speaks
    B. differences of opinion among the group members concerning the definition of terms
    C. a discussion leader who uses "openings" to get the discussion started
    D. a discussion leader who provides all suggestions and definitions for the group

———

TEST 3

DIRECTIONS: Questions 1 through 4 are to be answered *SOLELY* on the basis of the following information.

The insects you will control are just a minute fraction of the millions which inhabit the world. Man does well to hold his own in the face of the constant pressures that insects continue to exert upon him. Not only are the total numbers tremendous, but the number of individual kinds, or species, certainly exceeds 800,000 — number greater than that of all other animals combined. Many of these are beneficial but some are especially competitive with man. Not only are insects numerous, but they are among he most adaptable of all animals. In their many forms, they are fitted for almost any specific way of life. Their adaptability, combined with their tremendous rate of reproduction, gives insects an unequaled potential for survival!

The food of insects includes almost anything that can be eaten by any other animal as well as many things which cannot even be digested by any other animals. Most insects do not harm the products of man or carry diseases harmful to him; however many do carry diseases and others feed on his food and manufactured goods. Some are adapted to living only in open areas while others are able to live in extremely confined spaces. All of these factors combined make the insects a group of animals having many members which are a nuisance to man and thus of great importance.

The control of insects requires an understanding of their way of life. Thus it is necessary to understand the anatomy of the insect, its method of growth, the time it takes for the insect to grow from egg to adult, its habits, the stage of its life history in which it causes damage, its food, and its common living places. In order to obtain the best control, it is especially important to be able to identify correctly the specific insect involved because, without this knowledge, it is impossible to prescribe a proper treatment.

1. Which one of the following is a CORRECT statement about the insect population of the world, according to the above paragraph? The   1._____

    A. total number of insects is less than the total number of all other animals combined
    B. number of species of insects is greater than the number of species of all other animals combined
    C. total number of harmful insects is greater than the total number of those which are not harmful
    D. number of species of harmless insects is less than the number of species of those which are harmful

2. Insects will be controlled MOST efficiently if you   2._____

    A. understand why the insects are so numerous
    B. know what insects you are dealing with
    C. see if the insects compete with man
    D. are able to identify the food which the insects digest

3. According to the above passage, insects are of importance to a scientist PRIMARILY   3.___
   because they

    A. can be annoying, destructive, and harmful to man
    B. are able to thrive in very small spaces
    C. cause damage during their growth stages
    D. are so adaptable that they can adjust to any environment

4. According to the above passage, insects can eat   4.___

    A. everything that any other living thing can eat
    B. man's food and things which he makes
    C. anything which other animals can't digest
    D. only food and food products

———————

TEST 4

Questions 1-4.

DIRECTIONS: Answer Questions 1 through 4 on the basis of the information given in the following passage.

Telephone service in a government agency should be adequate and complete with respect to information given or action taken. It must be remembered that telephone contacts should receive special consideration since the caller cannot see the operator. People like to feel that they are receiving personal attention and that their requests or criticisms are receiving individual rather than routine consideration. All this contributes to what has come to be known as *tone of service*. The aim is to use standards which are clearly very good or superior. The factors to be considered in determining what makes good tone of service are speech, courtesy, understanding and explanations. A caller's impression of tone of service will affect the general public attitude toward the agency and city services in general.

1. The above passage states that people who telephone a government agency like to feel   1._____
    that they are

    A.   creating a positive image of themselves
    B.   being given routine consideration
    C.   receiving individual attention
    D.   setting standards for telephone service

2. Which of the following is NOT mentioned in the above passage as a factor in determining   2._____
    good tone of service?

    A.   Courtesy   B.   Education   C.   Speech   D.   Understanding

3. The above passage implies that failure to properly handle telephone calls is *most likely* to   3._____
    result in

    A.   a poor impression of city agencies by the public
    B.   a deterioration of courtesy toward operators
    C.   an effort by operators to improve the Tone of Service
    D.   special consideration by the public of operator difficulties

───────

TEST 5

Questions 1-5.

DIRECTIONS: Answer Questions 1 through 5 only on the basis of the information provided in the following passage:

For some office workers it is useful to be familiar with the four main classes of domestic mail; for others it is essential. Each class has a different rate of postage and some have requirements concerning wrapping, sealing or special information to be placed on the package.

First-class mail, the class which may not be opened for postal inspection, includes letters, post cards, business reply cards, and other kinds of written matter. There are different rates for some of the kinds of cards which can be sent by first-class mail. The maximum weight for an item sent by first-class mail is 70 pounds. An item which is not letter size should be marked "First Class" on all sides.

Although office workers most often come into contact with first-class mail, they may find it helpful to know something about the other classes. Second-class mail is generally used for mailing newspapers and magazines. Publishers of these articles must meet certain U.S. Postal Service requirements in order to obtain a permit to use second-class mailing rates. Third-class mail, which must weigh less than 1 pound, includes printed materials and merchandise parcels. There are two rate structures for this class, a single-piece rate and a bulk rate. Fourth-class mail, also known as parcel post, includes packages weighing from one to 40 pounds. For more information about these classes of mail and the actual mailing rates, contact your local post office.

1.   According to this passage, first-class mail is the only class which   1.___

   A.   has a limit on the maximum weight of an item
   B.   has different rates for items within the class
   C.   may not be opened for postal inspection
   D.   should be used by office workers

2.   According to this passage, the one of the following items which may CORRECTLY be sent by fourth-class mail is a   2.___

   A.   magazine weighing one-half pound
   B.   package weighing one-half pound
   C.   package weighing two pounds
   D.   post card

3.   According to this passage, there are different postage rates for   3.__

   A.   a newspaper sent by second-class mail and a magazine sent by second-class mail
   B.   each of the classes of mail
   C.   each pound of fourth-class mail
   D.   printed material sent by third-class mail and merchandise parcels sent by third-class mail

4. In order to send a newspaper by second-class mail, a publisher must   4._____

    A. have met certain postal requirements and obtained a permit
    B. indicate whether he wants to use the single-piece or the bulk rate
    C. make certain that the newspaper weighs less than one pound
    D. mark the newspaper "Second Class" on the top and bottom of the wrapper

5. Of the following types of information the one which is NOT mentioned in the passage is   5._____
the

    A. class of mail to which parcel post belongs
    B. kinds of items which can be sent by each class of mail
    C. maximum weight for an item sent by fourth-class mail
    D. postage rate for each of the four classes of mail

_____

TEST 6

Questions 1-5.

DIRECTIONS: Questions numbered 1 to 5 inclusive are to be answered in accordance with the following paragraph.

The thickness of insulation necessary for the most economical results varies with the steam temperature. The standard covering consists of 85 percent magnesia with 10 percent of long-fibre asbestos as a binder. Both matnesia and laminated asbestos-felt and other forms of mineral wool including glass wool are also used for heat insulation. The magnesia and laminated-asbestos coverings may be safely used at temperatures up to 600° F. Pipe insulation is applied in molded sections 3 feet long; the sections are attached to the pipe by means of galvanized iron wire or netting. Flanges and fittings can be insulated by direct application of magnesia cement to the metal without *reinforcement*. Insulation should always be maintained in good condition because it saves fuel. Routine maintenance of warm-pipe insulation should include prompt repair of damaged surfaces. Steam and hot-water leaks concealed by insulation will be difficult to detect. Underground steam or hot-water pipes are best insulated using a concrete trench with removable cover.

1. The word *reinforcement*, as used above, means, most nearly,   1.___

   A. resistance   B. strengthening   C. regulation   D. removal

2. According to the above paragraph, magnesia and laminated asbestos coverings may be   2.___
   safely used at temperatures up to

   A. 800° F   B. 720° F   C. 675° F   D. 600° F

3. According to the above paragraph, insulation should *always* be maintained in good con-   3.___
   dition because it

   A. is laminated   B. saves fuel
   C. is attached to the pipe   D. prevents leaks

4. According to the above paragraph, pipe insulation sections are attached to the pipe by   4.___
   means of

   A. binders   B. mineral wool
   C. netting   D. staples

5. According to the above paragraph, a leak in a hot-water pipe may be difficult to detect   5.___
   because, when insulation is used, the leak is

   A. underground   B. hidden
   C. routine   D. cemented

TEST 7

DIRECTIONS: Questions 1 to 4 inclusive are to be answered *only* in accordance with the following paragraph.

Cylindrical surfaces are the most common form of finished surfaces found on machine parts, although flat surfaces are also very common; hence, many metal-cutting *processes* are for the purpose of producing either cylindrical or flat surfaces. The machines used for cylindrical or flat shapes may be, and often are, utilized also for forming the various irregular or special shapes required on many machine parts. Because of the prevalence of cylindrical and flat surfaces, the student of manufacturing practice should learn first about the machines and methods employed to produce these surfaces. The cylindrical surfaces may be internal as in holes and cylinders. Any one part may, of course, have cylindrical sections of different diameters and lengths and include flat ends or shoulders and, frequently, there is a threaded part or, possibly, some finished surface that is not circular in cross-section. The prevalence of cylindrical surfaces on machine parts explains why lathes are found in all machine shops. It is important to understand the various uses of the lathe because many of the operations are the same fundamentally as those performed on other types of machine tools.

1.   According to the above paragraph, the *most common* form of finished surfaces found on machine parts is   1._____

   A.   cylindrical   B.   elliptical
   C.   flat   D.   square

2.   According to the above paragraph, *any one* part of cylindrical surfaces may have   2._____

   A.   chases   B.   shoulders   C.   keyways   D.   splines

3.   According to the above paragraph, lathes are found in all machine shops because cylindrical surfaces on machine parts are   3._____

   A.   scarce   B.   internal   C.   common   D.   external

4.   As used in the above paragraph, the word *processes* means   4._____

   A.   operations   B.   purposes   C.   devices   D.   tools

TEST 8

Questions 1-2.

DIRECTIONS: Questions 1 and 2 are to be answered in accordance with the following paragraph.

The principle of interchangeability requires manufacture to such specification that component parts of a device may be selected at random and assembled to fit and operate satisfactorily. Interchangeable manufacture, therefore, requires that parts be made to definite limits of error, and to fit gages instead of mating parts. Interchangeability does not necessarily involve a high degree of precision; stove lids, for example, are interchangeable but are not particularly accurate, and carriage bolts and nuts are not precision products but are completely interchangeable. Interchangeability may be employed in unit-production as well as mass-production systems of manufacture.

1.   According to the above paragraph, in order for parts to be interchangeable, they must be   1.___

    A.   precision-machined   B.   selectively-assembled
    C.   mass-produced   D.   made to fit gages

2.   According to the above paragraph, carriage bolts are interchangeable because they are   2.___

    A.   precision-made
    B.   sized to specific tolerances
    C.   individually matched products
    D.   produced in small units

KEY (CORRECT ANSWERS)

TEST 1	TEST 2	TEST 3	TEST 4	TEST 5	TEST 6	TEST 7	TEST 8
1. D	1. D	1. B	1. C	1. C	1. B	1. A	1. D
2. A	2. A	2. B	2. B	2. C	2. D	2. B	2. B
3. A	3. D	3. A	3. A	3. B	3. B	3. C	
4. C		4. B		4. A	4. C	4. A	
5. A				5. D	5. B		

READING COMPREHENSION
UNDERSTANDING WRITTEN MATERIALS

COMMENTARY

The ability to read and understand written materials – texts, publications, newspapers, orders, directions, expositions – is a skill basic to a functioning democracy and to an efficient business or viable government.

That is why almost all examinations – for beginning, middle, and senior levels – test reading comprehension, directly or indirectly.

The reading test measures how well you understand what you read. This is how it is done: You read a passage followed by several statements. From these statements, you choose the *one* statement, or answer, that is *BEST* supported by, or *BEST* matches, what is said in the paragraph. *PRINT THE LETTER OF THE CORRECT ANSWER IN THE SPACE AT THE RIGHT.*

SAMPLE QUESTIONS

DIRECTIONS: Answer Questions 1 to 2 *only* according to the information given in the following passage.

When a fingerprint technician inks and takes rolled impressions of a subject's fingers, the degree of downward pressure the technician applies is important. The correct pressure may best be determined through experience and observation. It is quite important, however, that the subject be cautioned to relax and not help the fingerprint technician by also applying pressure, as this prevents the fingerprint technician from gaging the amount needed. A method which is helpful in getting the subject to relax his hand is to instruct him to look at some distant object and not to look at his hands.

1. According to this passage, the technician tries to relax the subject's hands by   1._____

    A. instructing him to let his hands hang loosely
    B. telling him that being fingerprinted is painless
    C. asking him to look at his hand instead of some distant object
    D. asking him to look at something other than his hand

2. The subject is asked *NOT* to press down on his fingers while being fingerprinted because   2._____

    A. the impressions taken become rolled
    B. the subject may apply too little downward pressure and spoil the impressions
    C. the technician cannot tell whether he is applying the right degree of pressure
    D. he doesn't have the experience to apply the exact amount of pressure

CORRECT ANSWERS
    1. D
    2. C

EXAMINATION SECTION
TEST 1

Questions 1-3.

DIRECTIONS: The following three questions relate to the information given in the paragraph below.

Thermostats should be tested in hot water for proper opening. A bucket should be filled with sufficient water to cover the thermostat and fitted with a thermometer suspended in the water so that the sensitive bulb portion does not rest directly on the bucket. The water is then heated on a stove. As the temperature of the water passes the 160-165° range, the thermostat should start to open and should be completely opened when the temperature has risen to 185-190°. Lifting the thermostat into the air should cause a pronounced closing action and the unit should be closed entirely within a short time.

1. The thermostat described above is a device which opens and closes with changes in the   1.____

    A. position   B. pressure   C. temperature   D. surroundings

2. According to the above paragraph, the closing action of the thermostat should be tested   2.____
by

    A. working the thermostat back and forth
    B. permitting the water to cool gradually
    C. adding cold water to the bucket
    D. removing the thermostat from the bucket

3. The bulb of the thermometer should not rest directly on the bucket because   3.____

    A. the bucket gets hotter than the water
    B. the thermometer might be damaged in that position
    C. it is difficult to read the thermometer in that position
    D. the thermometer might interfere with operation of the thermostat

———

TEST 2

Questions 1-3.

DIRECTIONS: Questions 1 to 3 inclusive are to be answered in accordance with information given in the paragraph below.

All idle pumps should be turned daily by hand, and should be run under power at least once a week. Whenever repairs are made on a pump, a record should be kept so that it will be possible to judge the success with which the pump is performing its functions. If a pump fails to deliver liquid there may be an obstruction in the suction line, the pump's parts may be badly worn, or the packing defective.

1. According to the above paragraph, pumps   1._____

   A. in use should be turned by hand every day
   B. which are not in use should be run under power every day
   C. which are in daily use should be run under power several times a week
   D. which are not in use should be turned by hand every day

2. According to the above paragraph, the reason for keeping records of repairs made on   2._____
   pumps is to

   A. make certain that proper maintenance is being performed
   B. discover who is responsible for improper repairs
   C. rate the performance of the pumps
   D. know when to replace worn parts

3. The one of the following causes of pump failure which is *NOT* mentioned in the above   3._____
   paragraph is

   A. excessive suction lift   B. clogged lines
   C. bad packing   D. worn parts

_____

TEST 3

Questions 1-5.

DIRECTIONS: Answer Questions 1 through 5 *SOLELY* on the basis of the information contained in the following passage.

Floors in warehouses, storerooms, and shipping rooms must be strong enough to stay level under heavy loads. Unevenness of floors may cause boxes of materials to topple and fall. Safe floor load capacities and maximum heights to which boxes may be stacked should be posted conspicuously so all can notice it. Where material in boxes, containers, or cartons of the same weight is regularly stored, it is good practice to paint a horizontal line on the wall indicating the maximum height to which the material may be piled. A qualified expert should determine floor load capacity from the building plans, the age and condition of the floor supports, the type of floor, and other related information.

Working aisles are those from which material is placed into and removed from storage. Working aisles are of two types: transportation aisles, running the length of the building, and cross aisles, running across the width of the building. Deciding on the number, width, and location of working aisles is important. While aisles are necessary and determine boundaries of storage areas, they reduce the space actually used for storage.

1. According to the passage above, how should safe floor load capacities be made known to employees? They should be   1.___

    A. given out to each employee
    B. given to supervisors only
    C. printed in large red letters
    D. posted so that they are easily seen

2. According to the passage above, floor load capacities should be determined by   2.___

    A. warehouse supervisors   B. the fire department
    C. qualified experts   D. machine operators

3. According to the above passage, transportation aisles   3.___

    A. run the length of the building
    B. run across the width of the building
    C. are wider than cross aisles
    D. are shorter than cross aisles

4. According to the above passage, working aisles tend to   4.___

    A. take away space that could be used for storage
    B. add to space that could be used for storage
    C. slow down incoming stock
    D. speed up outgoing stock

5. According to the passage above, unevenness of floors may cause   5.___

    A. overall warehouse deterioration
    B. piles of stock to fall
    C. materials to spoil
    D. many worker injuries

TEST 4

DIRECTIONS: Questions 1 to 3 are to be answered *SOLELY* on the basis of the information contained in the following paragraph.

In a retail establishment, any overweight means a distinct loss to the merchant, and even an apparently inconsequential overweight on a single package or sale, when multiplied by the total number of transactions, could run into large figures. In addition to the use of reliable scales and weights, and their maintenance in proper condition, there must be proper supervision of the selling force. Such supervision is a difficult matter, particularly on the score of carelessness, as the depositing of extra amounts of material on the scale and failure to remove the same when it overbalances the scale may become a habit. In case of underweight, either in the weighing or by the use of fraudulent scales and weights, the seller soon will hear of it, but there is no reason why the amount weighed out should be in excess of what the customer pays for. Checking sales records against invoices and inventories can supply some indication of the tendency of the sales force to become careless in this field.

1.   Of the following, the *MOST* valid implication of the above paragraph is that   1._____

   A.   all overweights which occur in retail stores are in small amounts
   B.   even-arm and uneven-arm balances and weights which are unreliable lead more often to underweights than to overweights
   C.   overweights due to errors of salesclerks necessarily lead to large losses by a retailer
   D.   supervision to prevent overweights is more important to a retailer than remedial measures after their occurrence

2.   Of the following, the *MOST* valid implication of the above paragraph is that   2._____

   A.   depositing of insufficient amounts of commodities on scales and failure to add to them may become a habit with salesclerks
   B.   salesclerks should be trained in understanding and maintenance of scale mechanisms
   C.   supervision of salesclerks to prevent careless habits in weighing must depend upon personal observation
   D.   training and supervision of salesclerks in proper estimation of the amount asked for by the customer can eliminate errors of overweight

3.   According to the above paragraph, the *MOST* accurate of the following statements is: 3._____

   A.   For the most part, the ideas expressed in the paragraph do not apply to wholesale establishments.
   B.   Inventories of commodities prepacked in the store are the only ones which can be used in checking losses due to overweight.
   C.   Invoices which give the value and weight of merchandise received are useful in checking losses due to overweights.
   D.   The principal value of inventories is to indicate losses due to overweights.

─────────

TEST 5

Questions 1-5.

DIRECTIONS: Read *the* information below carefully. Then answer Questions 1 to 5 *SOLELY* on the basis of this information.

TITANIC AIR COMPRESSOR

Valves: The compressors are equipped with Titanic plate valves which are automatic in operation. Valves are so constructed that an entire valve assembly can readily be removed from the head. The valves provide large port areas with short lift and are accurately guided to Insure positive seating.

Starting Unloader: Each compressor (or air end) is equipped with a centrifugal governor which is bolted directly to the compressor crank shaft. The governor actuates cylinder relief valves so as to relieve pressure from the cylinders during starting and stopping. The motor is never required to start the compressor tinder load.

Air Strainer: Each cylinder air inlet connection is fitted with a suitable combination air strainer and muffler.

Pistons: Pistons are light-weight castings, ribbed internally to secure strength, and are accurately turned and ground. Each piston is fitted with four (4) rings, two of which are oil control rings. Piston pins are hardened and tempered steel of the full floating type. Bronze bushings are used between piston pin and piston.

Connecting Rods: Connecting rods are of solid bronze designed for maximum strength, rigidity and wear. Crank pins are fitted with renewable steel bushings. Connecting rods are of the one-piece type, there being no bolts, nuts, or cotter pins which can come loose. With this type of construction, wear is reduced to a negligible amount, and adjustment of wrist pin and crank pin bearings is unnecessary .

Main Bearings: Main bearings are of the ball type and are securely held in position by spacers. This type of bearing entirely eliminates the necessity of frequent adjustment or attention. The crank shaft is always in perfect alignment.

Crank Shaft: The crank shaft is a one-piece heat-treated forging of best quality open-hearth steel, of rugged design and of sufficient size to transmit the motor power and any additional stresses which may occur in service. Each crank shaft is counter-balanced Cdynamically balanced) to reduce vibration to a minimum, and is accurately machined to properly receive the ball-bearing races, crank pin bushing, flexible coupling, and centrifugal governor. Suitable provision is made to insure proper lubrication of all crank shaft bearings and bushings with the minimum amount of attention.

Coupling: Compressor and motor shafts are connected through a Morse Chain Company all-metal enclosed flexible coupling. This coupling consists of two sprockets, one mounted on, and keyed to, each shaft; the sprockets are wrapped by a single Morse Chain, the entire assembly being enclosed in a split aluminum grease-packed cover. . ..

1.   The crank pin of the connecting rod is fitted with a renewable bushing made of   1.___

   A.   solid bronze
   B.   steel
   C.   a light-weight casting
   D.   ball bearings

2.   When the connecting rod is of the one-piece type,   2.___

   A.   the wrist pins require frequent adjustment
   B.   the crank pins require frequent adjustment

C. the cotter pins frequently will come loose
D. wear is reduced to a negligible amount

3. The centrifugal governor is bolted *directly* to the   3._____

    A. compressor crank shaft   B. main bearing
    C. piston pin   D. muffler

4. The *number* of oil control rings required for each piston is   4._____

    A. one   B. two   C. three   D. four

5. The compressor and motor shafts are connected through a flexible coupling. These cou-   5._____
plings are

    A. keyed to the shafts
    B. brazed to the shafts
    C. soldered to the shafts
    D. press-fit to the shafts

TEST 6

Questions 1-6.

DIRECTIONS: Answer Questions 1 to 6 *only* according to the information given in the paragraph below.

Perhaps the strongest argument the mass transit backer has is the advantage in efficiency that mass transit has over the automobile in the urban traffic picture. It has been estimated that given comparable location and construction conditions, the subway can carry four
times as many passengers per hour and cost half as much to build as urban highways. Yet
public apathy regarding the mass transportation movement in the 1960's resulted in the building of more roads. Planned to provide 42,000 miles of highways in the period from 1956-72,
including 7500 miles within cities, the Federal Highway System project is now about two-
thirds completed. The Highway Trust Fund supplies 90 percent of the cost of the System, with
state and local sources putting up the rest of the money. By contrast, a municipality has had
to put up the bulk of the cost of a rapid transit system. Although the System and its Trust Fund
have come under attack in the past few years from environmentalists and groups opposed to
the continued building of urban freeways – considered to be the most expensive, destructive,
and inefficient segments of the System – a move by them to get the Trust Fund transformed
into a general transportation fund at the expiration of the present program in 1972 seems to
be headed nowhere.

1. Given similar building conditions and location, a city that builds a subway instead of a   1.___
   highway can expect to receive for each dollar spent

   A. half as much transport value
   B. twice as much transport value
   C. four times as much transport value
   D. eight times as much transport value

2. The general attitude of the public in the past ten years toward the mass transportation   2.___
   movement has been

   A. favorable   B. indifferent
   C. enthusiastic   D. unfriendly

3. The number of miles of highways still to be completed in the Federal Highway System   3.___
   project is, most nearly,

   A. 2,500   B. 5,000   C. 14,000   D. 28,000

4. *What* do certain groups who object to some features of the Federal Highway System pro-   4.___
   gram want to do with the Highway Trust Fund after 1972?

   A. Extend it in order to complete the project
   B. Change it so that the money can be used for all types of transportation
   C. End it even if the project is not completed
   D. Change it so that the money will be used only for urban freeways

5. *Which one* of the following statements is a *VALID* conclusion based on the facts in the   5.___
   above passage?

A. The advantage of greater efficiency is the only argument that supporters of the mass transportation movement can offer.
B. It was easier for cities to build roads rather than mass transit systems in the last 15 years because of the large financial contribution made by the Federal Government.
C. Mass transit systems cause as much congestion and air pollution in cities as automobiles.
D. In 1972, the Highway Trust Fund becomes a general transportation fund.

6. The *MAIN* idea or theme of the above passage is that the   6.____

A. cost of the Federal Highway System is shared by the federal, state, and local governments
B. public is against spending money for building mass transportation facilities in the cities
C. cities would benefit more from expansion and improvement of their mass transit systems than from the building of more highways
D. building of mass transportation facilities has been slowed by the Highway Trust Fund

---

TEST 7

Questions 1-5.

DIRECTIONS: Answer Questions 1 to 5 *ONLY* according to the information given in the paragraph below.

The use of role-playing as a training technique was developed during the past decade by social scientists, particularly psychologists, who have been active in training experiments. Originally, this technique was applied by clinical psychologists who discovered that a patient appears to gain understanding of an emotionally disturbing situation when encouraged to act out roles in that situation. As applied in government and business organizations, the purpose of role-playing is to aid employees to understand certain work problems involving interpersonal relations and to enable observers to evaluate various reactions to them. Thus, for example, on the problem of handling grievances, two individuals from the group might be selected to act out extemporaneously the parts of subordinate and supervisor. When this situation is enacted by various pairs among the class and the techniques and results are discussed, the members of the group are presumed to reach conclusions about the most effective means of handling similar situations. Often the use of role reversal, where participants take parts different from their actual work roles, assists individuals to gain more insight into other people's problems and viewpoints. Although role-playing can be a rewarding training device, the trainer must be aware of his responsibilities. If this technique is to be successful, thorough briefing of both actors and observers as to the situation in question, the participants' roles, and what to look for, is essential.

1. The role-playing technique was *FIRST* used for the purpose of   1.___

   A. measuring the effectiveness of training programs
   B. training supervisors in business organizations
   C. treating emotionally disturbed patients
   D. handling employee grievances

2. When role-playing is used in private business as a training device, the *CHIEF* aim is to   2.___

   A. develop better relations between supervisor and subordinate in the handling of grievances
   B. come up with a solution to a specific problem that has arisen
   C. determine the training needs of the group
   D. increase employee understanding of the human-relation factors in work situations

3. From the above passage, it is *MOST* reasonable to conclude that when role-playing is used, it is preferable to have the roles acted out by   3.___

   A. only one set of actors
   B. no more than two sets of actors
   C. several different sets of actors
   D. the trainer or trainers of the group

4. It can be *inferred* from the above passage that a limitation of role-play as a training method is that   4._

   A. many work situations do not lend themselves to role-play
   B. employees are not experienced enough as actors to play the roles realistically
   C. only trainers who have psychological training can use it successfully
   D. participants who are observing and not acting do not benefit from it

5. To obtain *good* results from the use of role-play in training, a trainer should give participants

    A. a minimum of information about the situation so that they can act spontaneously
    B. scripts which illustrate the best method for handling the situation
    C. a complete explanation of the problem and the roles to be acted out
    D. a summary of work problems which involve interpersonal relations

5.____

KEY (CORRECT ANSWERS)

TEST 1

1. C
2. D
3. A

TEST 2

1. A
2. C
3. A

TEST 3

1. D
2. C
3. A
4. A
5. B

TEST 4

1. D
2. C
3. C

TEST 5

1. B
2. D
3. A
4. B
5. A

TEST 6

1. D
2. B
3. C
4. B
5. B
6. C

TEST 7

1. C
2. D
3. C
4. A
5. C

READING COMPREHENSION
UNDERSTANDING AND INTERPRETING WRITTEN MATERIAL
EXAMINATION SECTION
TEST 1

DIRECTIONS: All questions are to be answered *SOLELY* on the basis of the information contained in the passage. Each question or incomplete statement is followed by several suggested answers or completions. Select the one that *BEST* answers the question or completes the statement. *PRINT THE LETTER OF THE CORRECT ANSWER IN THE SPACE AT THE RIGHT.*

Questions 1-3.

The equipment in a mail room may include a mail-metering machine. This machine simultaneously stamps, postmarks, seals, and counts letters as fast as the operator can feed them. It can also print the proper postage directly on a gummed strip to be affixed to bulky items. It is equipped with a meter which is removed from the machine and sent to the postmaster to be set for a given number of stampings of any denomination. The setting of the meter must be paid for in advance. One of the advantages of metered mail is that it bypasses the cancellation operation and, thereby, facilitates handling by the post office. Mail metering also makes the pilfering of stamps impossible, but does not prevent the passage of personal mail in company envelopes through the meters unless there is established a rigid control or censorship over outgoing mail.

1.   According to this statement, the postmaster   1._____

   A.   is responsible for training new clerks in the use of mail-metering machines
   B.   usually recommends that both large and small firms adopt the use of mail metering machines
   C.   is responsible for setting the meter to print a fixed number of stampings
   D.   examines the mail-metering machines to see that they are properly installed in the mail room

2.   According to this statement, the use of mail-metering machines   2._____

   A.   requires the employment of more clerks in a mail room than does the use of postage stamps
   B.   interferes with the handling of large quantities of out-going mail
   C.   does not prevent employees from sending their personal letters at company expense
   D.   usually involves smaller expenditures for mail-room equipment than does the use of postage stamps

3.   On the basis of this statement, it is MOST accurate to state that   3._____

   A.   mail-metering machines are often used for opening envelopes
   B.   postage stamps are generally used when bulky packages are to be mailed
   C.   the use of metered mail tends to interfere with rapid mail handling by the post office
   D.   mail-metering machines can seal and count letters at the same time

Questions 4-8.

It is the Housing Administration's policy that all tenants, whether new or transferring from one housing development to another, shall be required to pay a standard security deposit of one month's rent based on the rent at the time of admission. There are, however, certain exceptions to this policy. Employees of the Administration shall not be required to pay a security deposit if they secure an apartment in an Administration development. Where the payment of a full security deposit may present a hardship to a tenant, the development's manager may allow a tenant to move into an apartment upon payment of only part of the security deposit. In such cases, however, the tenant must agree to gradually pay the balance of the deposit. If a tenant transfers from one apartment to another within the same project, the security deposit originally paid by the tenant for his former apartment will be acceptable for his new apartment, even if the rent in the new apartment is greater than the rent in the former one. Finally, tenants who receive public assistance need not pay a security deposit before moving into an apartment if the appropriate agency states, in writing, that it will pay the deposit. However, it is the responsibility of the development's manager to make certain that payment shall be received within one month of the date that the tenant moves into the apartment.

4. According to the above passage, when a tenant transfers from one apartment to another in the same development, the Housing Administration will   4.___

   A. *accept* the tenant's old security deposit as the security deposit for his new apartment regardless of the new apartment's rent
   B. *refund* the tenant's old security deposit and not requires him to pay a new deposit
   C. *keep* the tenant's old security deposit and require him to pay a new deposit
   D. *require* the tenant to pay a new security deposit based on the difference between his old rent and his new rent

5. On the basis of the above passage, it is INCORRECT to state that a tenant who receives public assistance may move into an Administration development if   5.___

   A. he pays the appropriate security deposit
   B. the appropriate agency gives a written indication that it will pay the security deposit before the tenant moves in
   C. the appropriate agency states, by telephone, that it will pay the security deposit
   D. he appropriate agency writes the manager to indicate that the security deposit will be paid within one month but not less than two weeks from the date the tenant moves into the apartment

6. On the basis of the above passage, a tenant who transfers from an apartment In one development to an apartment in a different development will   6._

   A. forfeits his old security deposit and be required to pay another deposit
   B. have his old security deposit refunded and not have to pay a new deposit
   C. pays the difference between his old security deposit and the new one
   D. has to pay a security deposit based on the new apartment's rent 2

7. The Housing Administration will NOT require payment of a Security deposit if a tenant 7.____

    A. is, an Administration employee
    B. is receiving public assistance
    C. claims that payment will present a hardship
    D. indicates, in writing, that he will be responsible for any damage done to his apartment

8. Of the following, the BEST title for the above passage is: 8.____

    A. Security Deposits - Transfers
    B. Security Deposits - Policy
    C. Exemptions and Exceptions - Security Deposits
    D. Amounts - Security Deposits

Questions 9-11.

Terrazzo flooring will last a very long time if it is cared for properly. Lacquers, shellac or varnish preparations should never be used on terrazzo. Soap cleaners are not recommended, since they dull the appearance of the floor. Alkaline solutions are harmful, so neutral cleaner or non-alkaline synthetic detergents will give best results. If the floor is very dirty, it may be necessary to scrub it. The same neutral cleaning solution should be used for scrubbing as for mopping. Scouring powder may be sprinkled at particularly dirty spots. Do not use steel wool for scrubbing. Small pieces of steel filings left on the floor will rust and discolor the terrazzo. Non-woven nylon or open-mesh fabric abrasive pads are suitable for scrubbing terrazzo floors.

9. According to the passage above, the BEST cleaning agent for terrazzo flooring is a(n) 9.____

    A. soap cleaner
    B. varnish preparation
    C. neutral cleaner
    D. alkaline solution

10. According to the passage above, terrazzo floors should NOT be scrubbed with 10.____

    A. non-woven nylon abrasive pads
    B. steel wool
    C. open-mesh fabric abrasive pads
    D. scouring powder

11. As used in the passage above, the word *discolor* means, most nearly, 11.____

    A. crack
    B. scratch
    C. dissolve
    D. stain

Questions 12-15.

Planning for the unloading of incoming trucks is not easy since generally little or no advance notice of truck arrivals is received. The height of the floor of truck bodies and loading platforms sometimes are different; this makes necessary the use of special unloading methods. When available, hydraulic ramps compensate for the differences in platform and truck floor levels. When hydraulic ramps are not available, forklift equipment can sometimes be used, if the truck springs are strong enough to support such equipment. In a situation like this, the unloading operation does not differ much from unloading a railroad box car In the cases where the forklift truck or a hydraulic pallet jack cannot be used inside the truck, a pallet dolly should be placed inside the truck, so that the empty pallet can be loaded close to the truck contents and rolled easily to the truck door and platform.

12. According to the passage above, unloading trucks are   12.___
    A. easy to plan since the time of arrival is usually known beforehand
    B. the same as loading a railroad box car
    C. hard to plan since trucks arrive without notice
    D. a very normal thing to do

13. According to the above passage, which materials-handling equipment can make up for   13.___
    the difference in platform and truck floor levels?
    A. Hydraulic jacks   B. Hydraulic ramps
    C. Forklift trucks   D. Conveyors

14. According to the passage above, what materials-handling equipment can be used when   14.__
    a truck cannot support the weight of forklift equipment?
    A. A pallet dolly   B. A hydraulic ramp
    C. Bridge plates   D. A warehouse tractor

15. Which is the BEST title for the above passage?   15.__
    A. Unloading Railroad Box Cars   B. Unloading Motor Trucks
    C. Loading Rail Box   D. Loading Motor Trucks

Questions 16-19.

    Ventilation, as used in fire-fighting operations, means opening up a building or structure
in which a fire is burning to release the accumulated heat, smoke, and gases. Lack of knowledge of the principles of ventilation on the part of firemen may result in unnecessary punishment due to ventilation being neglected or improperly handled. While ventilation itself
extinguishes no fires, when used in an intelligent manner, it allows firemen to get at the fire
more quickly, easily, and with less danger and hardship.

16. According to the above paragraph, the MOST important result of failure to apply the prin-   16._
    ciples of ventilation at a fire may be
    A. loss of public confidence   B. disciplinary action
    C. waste of water   D. excessive use of equipment
    E. injury to firemen

17. It may be inferred from the above paragraph that the CHIEF advantage of ventilation is   17._
    that it
    A. eliminates the need for gas masks
    B. reduces smoke damage
    C. permits firemen to work closer to the fire
    D. cools the fire
    E. enables firemen to use shorter hose lines

18. Knowledge of the principles of ventilation, as defined in the above paragraph, would be   18.
    LEAST important in a fire in a
    A. tenement house   B. grocery store
    C. ship's hold   D. lumberyard
    E. office building

19. We may conclude from the above paragraph that, for the well-trained and equipped fire-   19._____
     man, ventilation is

       A. a simple matter   B. rarely necessary
       C. relatively unimportant   D. a basic tool
       E. sometimes a handicap

Questions 20-22.

       Many public service and industrial organizations are becoming increasingly insistent that
supervisors at the work level be qualified instructors. The reason for this is that technological
improvements and overall organizational growth require the acquisition of new skills and
knowledge by workers. These skills and knowledge can be acquired in two ways. They can
be gained either by absorption-rubbing shoulders with the job or through planned instruction.
Permitting the acquisition of new skills and knowledge is to be haphazard and uncertain is too
costly. At higher supervisory levels, the need for instructing subordinates is not so obvious,
but it is just as important as at the lowest work level. A high-ranking supervisor accomplishes
the requirements of his position only if his subordinate supervisors perform their work efficiently. Regardless of one's supervisory position, the ability to instruct easily and efficiently
helps to insure well-qualified and thoroughly-trained subordinates. There exists an unfounded
but rather prevalent belief that becoming a competent instructor is a long, arduous, and complicated process. This belief arises partially as a result of the requirement of a long period of
college preparation involved in preparing teachers for our school system. This time is necessary because teachers must learn a great deal of subject matter. The worker who advances
to a supervisory position generally has superior skill and knowledge; therefore, he has only to
learn the techniques by which he can impart his knowledge in order to become a competent
instructor.

20. According to the above paragraph, a prolonged period of preparation for instructing is NOT   20._____
     generally necessary for a worker who is advanced to a supervisory position because

       A. he may already possess some of the requirements of a competent instructor
       B. his previous job knowledge is generally sufficient to enable him to begin instructing
           immediately
       C. in his present position there is less need for the specific job knowledge of the ordi-
           nary worker
       D. the ability to instruct follows naturally from superior skill and knowledge

21. According to the above paragraph, it is important for the higher-level supervisor to be a   21._____
     good instructor because

       A. at this level there is a tendency to overlook the need for instruction of both subordi-
           nate supervisors and workers
       B. good training practices will then be readily adopted by lower-level supervisors
       C. the need for effective training is more critical at the higher levels of responsibility
       D. training can be used to improve the supervisory performance of his subordinate
           supervisors

22. According to the above paragraph, the acquisition of new skills and knowledge by work-   22.__
ers is BEST accomplished when

    A. the method of training allows for the use of absorption
    B. organizational growth and technological improvement indicate a need for further
training
    C. such training is the result of careful planning
    D. the cost factor involved in training can be readily justified

Questions 23-25.

The organization of any large agency falls into three broad general zones: top management, middle management, and rank-and-file operations. The normal task of middle management is to supervise, direct and control the performance of operations within the scope of law,
policy, and regulations already established. Where policy is settled and well defined, middle
management is basically a set of standard operations, although they may call for high-devel-
oped skills. Where, however, policy is not clearly stated, is ambiguous, or is rapidly shifting,
middle management is likely to have an important influence upon emergency policy trends.
Persons working in the zone of middle management usually become specialists. They need
specialist knowledge of law, rules and regulations, and court decisions governing their organization if they are to discharge their duties effectively. They will also have acquired specialist
knowledge of relationships and sequences in the normal flow of business. Further, their
attention is brought to bear on a particular administrative task, in a particular jurisdiction, with
a particular clientele. The importance of middle management is obviously great. The reasons
for such importance are not difficult to find: Here it is that the essential action of government
in behalf of citizens is taken; here it is that citizens deal with government when they pass
beyond their first contacts; here is a training ground from which a considerable part of top
management emerges; and here also it is that the spirit and temper of the public service and
its reputation are largely made,

23. According to the above paragraph, the critical importance of middle management is due   23.
to the fact that it is at this level that

    A. formal executive training can be most useful
    B. the greatest amount of action is taken on the complaints of the general public
    C. the official actions taken have the greatest impact on general attitudes towards the
public service
    D. the public most frequently comes in contact with governmental operations and
agencies

24. According to the above paragraph, the one of the following statements which is NOT   24
offered as an explanation of the tendency for middle management responsibility to produce specialists is that

    A. middle-management personnel frequently feel that their work is the most important
in an organization
    B. specialized knowledge is acquired during the course of everyday work
    C. specialized knowledge is necessary for effective job performance
    D. their work assignments are directed to specific problems in specific situations

25. According to the above paragraph, the GREATEST impact of middle management in policy determination would be likely to be felt in the situation in which   25.____

    A.   middle management possesses highly developed operational skills
    B.   several policy directives from top management are subject to varying interpretations
    C.   the authority of middle management to supervise, direct, and control operations has been clearly established
    D.   top management has neglected to consider the policy views of middle management

-----

KEYS (CORRECT ANSWERS)

1.	C	11.	D
2.	C	12.	C
3.	D	13.	B
4.	A	14.	A
5.	C	15.	B
6.	D	16.	E
7.	A	17.	C
8.	B	18.	D
9.	C	19.	D
10.	B	20.	A

21.	D
22.	C
23.	C
24.	A
25.	B

TEST 2

Questions 1-2.

Metal spraying is used for many purposes. Worn bearings on shafts and spindles can be readily restored to original dimensions with any desired metal or alloy. Low-carbon steel shafts may be supplied with high-carbon steel journal surfaces, which can then be ground to size after spraying. By using babbitt wire, bearings can be lined or babbitted while rotating. Pump shafts and impellers can be coated with any desired metal to overcome wear and corrosion. Valve seats may be re-surfaced. Defective castings can be repaired by filling in blow-holes and checks. The application of metal spraying to the field of corrosion resistance is growing, although the major application in this field is in the use of sprayed zinc. tin, lead, and aluminum have been used considerably. The process is used for structural and tank applications in the field as well as in the shop.

1. According to the above paragraph, worn bearing surfaces on shafts are metal-sprayed in order to   1.__

   A. prevent corrosion of the shaft
   B. fit them into larger-sized impellers
   C. returns them to their original sizes
   D. replaces worn babbitt metal

2. According to the above paragraph, rotating bearings can be metal-sprayed using   2._

   A. babbitt wire   B. high-carbon steel
   C. low-carbon steel   D. any desired metal

Questions 3-5.

The method of cleaning which should generally be used is the space assignment method. Under this method, the buildings to be cleaned are divided into different sections. Within each section, each crew of Custodial Assistants is assigned to do one particular cleaning job. For example, within a section, one crew may be assigned to cleaning offices, another to scrubbing floors, a third to collecting trash, and so on. Other methods which may be used are the post-assignment method and the gang-cleaning method. Under the post-assignment method, a Custodial Assistant is assigned to one area of a building and performs all cleaning jobs in that area. This method is seldom used except where buildings are so small and distant from each other that it is not economical to use the space-assignment method. Under the gang-cleaning method, a Custodial Foreman takes a number of Custodial Assistants through a section of the building. These Custodial Assistants work as a group and complete the various cleaning jobs as they go. This method is generally used only where the building contains very large open areas.

3. According to the passage above, under the space-assignment method, each crew *generally*   3.

   A. works as a group and does a variety of different cleaning jobs
   B. is assigned to one area and performs all cleaning jobs in that area
   C. does one particular cleaning job within a section of a building
   D. follows the Custodial Foreman through a building containing large, open areas

4. According to the passage above, the post-assignment method is used mostly where the buildings to be cleaned are
4.____

    A. *large* in size and situated *close together*
    B. *small* in size and situated *close together*
    C. *large* in size and situated *far apart*
    D. *small* in size and situated *far apart*

5. As used in the passage above, the word *economical* means, most nearly,
5.____

    A. thrifty   B. agreed
    C. unusual   D. wasteful

Questions 6-9.

    The desirability of complete refuse collection by municipalities is becoming generally accepted. In many cases, however, such ideal service is economically impractical and certain limits must be imposed. Some municipal authorities find it necessary to regulate the quantity of refuse, by weight or volume, which will be collected from a single residence or place of business at one collection. The purpose of the regulations is twofold: First, to maintain the degree of service rendered on a somewhat uniform basis; and, second, to insure a more or less constant collection from week to week. If left unregulated, careless producers might permit large quantities of refuse to accumulate on their premises over long periods and place abnormal amounts out for collection at irregular intervals, thus upsetting the collection schedule. Regulation is especially applied to large wholesale, industrial, and manufacturing enterprises which, in the great majority of cases, are required to dispose of all or part of their refuse themselves, at their own expense. The maximum quantities permitted by regulation should obviously be sufficient to take care of a normal accumulation at a household over the established interval between regular collections. In commercial districts, the maximum quantity limitations are often fixed on arbitrary bases rather than on normal production.

6. According to the above paragraph, many municipalities do not have complete refuse collections because
6.____

    A. it costs too much   B. it is difficult to regulate
    C. it is not a municipal function   D. they don't consider it desirable

7. According to the above paragraph, regulation by municipalities of the amount of refuse collected per collection from any one place of business does NOT contribute to
7.____

    A. accumulation of refuse by careless producers
    B. maintenance of collection schedules
    C. steady collection from one week to the next
    D. uniform service

8. According to the above paragraph, regulations by municipalities of refuse collection from certain enterprises helps to cut down
8.____

    A. accumulation of refuse for private collection
    B. the amount of refuse produced
    C. variation in the volume of refuse produced
    D. variation in collection service

9. According to the above paragraph, municipalities limit the amount of refuse collected in commercial districts on an arbitrary basis rather than on the basis of a normal accumulation. This is *probably* done because   9.___

    A. arbitrary standards are easy to establish and enforce
    B. normal accumulation is different for each district
    C. normal accumulation would require the collection of too much refuse
    D. there is no such thing as a normal accumulation

Questions 10-13.

Modern office methods, geared to ever higher speeds and aimed at ever greater efficiency, are largely the result of the typewriter. The typewriter is a substitute for handwriting and, in the hands of a skilled typist, not only turns out letters and other documents at least three times faster than a penman can do the work, but turns out the greater volume more uniformly and legibly. With the use of carbon paper and onionskin paper, identical copies can be made at the same time.

The typewriter, besides its effect on the conduct of business and government, has had a very important effect on the position of women. The typewriter has done much to bring women into business and government and today there are vastly more women than men typists. Many women have used the keys of the typewriter to climb the ladder to responsible managerial positions.

The typewriter, as its name implies, employs type to make an ink impression on paper. For many years, the manual typewriter was the standard machine used. Today, the electric typewriter is dominant, and completely automatic typewriters are coming into wider use.

The mechanism of the office manual typewriter includes a set of keys arranged systematically in rows; a semicircular frame of type, connected to the keys by levers; the carriage, or paper carrier; a rubber roller, called a platen, against which the type strikes; and an inked ribbon which makes the impression of the type character when the key strikes it.

10. The passage mentions a number of good features of the combination of a skilled typist and a typewriter of the following, the feature which is NOT mentioned in the passage is   10.___

    A. speed   B. uniformity
    C. reliability   D. legibility

11. According to the passage, a skilled typist can   11.___

    A. turn out at least five carbon copies of typed matter
    B. type at least three times faster than a penman can write
    C. type more than 80 words a minute
    D. readily move into a managerial position

12. According to the passage, which of the following is NOT part of the mechanism of a manual typewriter?   12.___

    A. Carbon paper   B. Paper carrier
    C. Platen   D. Inked ribbon

13. According to the passage, the typewriter has helped   13.____

    A. men more than women in business
    B. women in career advancement into management
    C. men and women equally, but women have taken better advantage of it
    D. more women than men, because men generally dislike routine typing work

Questions 14-18.

Reductions in pipe size of a building heating system are made with eccentric fittings and are pitched downward. The ends of mains with gravity return shall be at least 18" above the water line of the boiler. As condensate flows opposite to the steam, run outs are one size larger than the vertical pipe and are pitched upward. In a one-pipe system, an automatic air vent must be provided at each main to relieve air pressure and to let steam enter the radiator. As steam enters the radiator, a *thermal* device causes the vent to close, thereby holding the steam. Steam mains should not be less than two inches in diameter. The end of the steam main should have a minimum size of one-half of its greatest diameter. Small steam systems should be sized for a 2-oz. pressure drop. Large steam systems should be sized for a 4-oz. pressure drop.

14. The word *thermal*, as used in the above paragraph, means, most nearly,   14.____

    A. convector   B. heat
    C. instrument   D. current

15. According to the above paragraph, the one of the following that is one size larger than   15.____
the vertical pipe is the

    A. steam main   B. valve
    C. water line   D. run out

16. According to the above paragraph, small steam systems should be sized for a pressure   16.____
drop of

    A. 2 oz   B. 3 oz
    C. 4 oz   D. 5 oz

17. According to the above paragraph ends of mains with gravity return shall be *at least*   17.____

    A. 18" above the water line of the boiler
    B. one-quarter of the greatest diameter of the main
    C. twice the size of the vertical pipe in the main
    D. 18" above the steam line of the boiler

18. According to the above paragraph, the one of the following that is provided at each main   18.____
to relieve air pressure is a (n)

    A. gravity return   B. convector
    C. eccentric   D. vent

Questions 19-21.

The bearings of all electrical equipment should be subjected to careful inspection at scheduled periodic intervals in order to secure maximum life. The newer type of sleeve bearings requires very little attention since the oil does not become contaminated and oil leakage is negligible. Maintenance of the correct oil level is frequently the only upkeep required for years of service with this type of bearing.

19. According to the above paragraph, the MAIN reason for making periodic inspections of electrical equipment is to   19.__

    A. reduce waste of lubricants
    B. prevent injury to operators
    C. make equipment last longer
    D. keeps operators "on their toes"

20. According to the above paragraph, the bearings of electrical equipment should be inspected   20.__

    A. whenever the equipment isn't working properly
    B. whenever there is time for inspections
    C. at least once a year
    D. at regular times

21. According to the above paragraph, when using the newer type of sleeve bearings,   21.__

    A. oil leakage is slight
    B. the oil level should be checked every few years
    C. oil leakage is due to carelessness
    D. oil soon becomes dirty

Questions 22-25.

There is hardly a city in the country that is not short of fire protection in some areas within its boundaries. These municipalities have spread out and have re-shuffled their residential, business and industrial districts without readjusting the existing protective fire forces; or creating new protection units. Fire stations are still situated according to the needs of earlier times and have not been altered or improved to house modern fire-fighting equipment. They are neither efficient for carrying out their tasks nor livable for the men who must occupy them.

22. Of the following, the title which BEST describes the central idea of the above paragraph is: 22.__

    A. The Dynamic Nature of Contemporary Society
    B. The Cost of Fire Protection
    C. The Location and Design of Fire Stations
    D. The Design and Use of Fire-Fighting Equipment
    E. The Growth of American Cities

23. According to the above paragraph, fire protection is inadequate in the United States in   23.

    A. most areas of some cities   B. some areas of most cities
    C. some areas in all cities   D. all areas in some cities
    E. most areas in most cities

24. The one of the following criteria for planning of fire stations which is NOT mentioned in the above paragraph is: 24.____

    A. Comfort of firemen   B. Proper location
    C. Design for modern equipment   D. Efficiency of operation
    E. Cost of construction

25. Of the following suggestions for improving the fire service, the *one* which would BEST   25.____
    deal with the problem discussed in the paragraph above would involve

    A. specialized training in the use of modern fire apparatus
    B. replacement of obsolete fire apparatus
    C. revision of zoning laws
    D. longer basic training for probationary firemen
    E. reassignment of fire districts

Questions 26-30.

Stopping, standing, and parking of motor vehicles is regulated by law to keep the public highways open for a smooth flow of traffic, and to keep stopped vehicles from blocking intersections, driveways, signs, fire hydrants, and other areas that must be kept clear. These established regulations apply in all situations, unless otherwise indicated by signs. Other local restrictions are posted in the areas to which they apply. Three examples of these other types of restrictions, which may apply singly or in combination with one another are:
NO STOPPING - This means that a driver may not stop a vehicle for any purpose except when necessary to avoid interference with other vehicles, or in compliance with directions of a police officer or signal.
NO STANDING - This means that a driver may stop a vehicle only temporarily to actually receive or discharge passengers.
NO PARKING - This means that a driver may stop a vehicle only temporarily to actually load or unload merchandise or passengers. When stopped, it is advisable to turn on warning flashers if equipped with them. However, one should never use a directional signal for this purpose, because it may confuse other drivers. Some NO PARKING signs prohibit parking between certain hours on certain days. For example, the sign may read NO PARKING 8 a.m. to 11 a.m., MONDAY, WEDNESDAY, FRIDAY. These signs are usually utilized on streets where cleaning operations take place on alternate days.

26. The parking regulation that applies to fire hydrants is an example of   26.____

    A. local regulations   B. established regulations
    C. posted regulations   D. temporary regulations

27. When stopped in a NO PARKING zone, it is advisable to   27.____

    A. turn on the right directional signal to indicate to other drivers that you will remain stopped
    B. turn on the left directional signal to indicate to other drivers that you may be leaving the curb after a period of time
    C. turn on the warning flashers if your car is equipped with them
    D. put the vehicle in reverse so that the backup lights will be on to warn approaching cars that you have temporarily stopped

28. You may stop a vehicle temporarily to discharge passengers in an area under the restriction of a   28.___

    A. NO STOPPING - NO STANDING zone
    B. NO STANDING - NO PARKING zone
    C. NO PARKING - NO STOPPING zone
    D. NO STOPPING - NO STANDING - NO PARKING zone

29. A sign reads "NO PARKING 8 a.m. to 11 a.m., MONDAY, WEDNESDAY, FRIDAY." Based   29.___
on this sign, an enforcement agent would issue a summons to a car that is parked on a

    A. Tuesday at 9:30 a.m.   B. Wednesday at 12:00.a.m.
    C. Friday at 10:30 a.m.   D. Saturday at 8:00 a.m.

30. NO PARKING signs prohibiting parking between certain hours, on certain days, are usually utilized on streets where   30.___

    A. vehicles frequently take on and discharge passengers
    B. cleaning operations take place on alternate days
    C. NO STOPPING signs have been ignored
    D. commercial vehicles take on and unload merchandise

KEYS (CORRECT ANSWERS)

1.	C	16.	A
2.	A	17.	A
3.	C	18.	D
4.	D	19.	C
5.	A	20.	D
6.	A	21.	A
7.	A	22.	C
8.	D	23.	B
9.	C	24.	E
10.	C	25.	E
11.	B	26.	B
12.	A	27.	C
13.	B	28.	B
14.	B	29.	C
15.	D	30.	B

READING COMPREHENSION
UNDERSTANDING AND INTERPRETING WRITTEN MATERIAL
TEST 1

DIRECTIONS: Each question or incomplete statement is followed by several suggested answers or completions. Select the one that BEST answers the question or completes the statement. *PRINT THE LETTER OF THE CORRECT ANSWER IN THE SPACE AT THE RIGHT.*

DIRECTIONS FOR THIS SECTION:
        All questions are to be answered SOLELY on the basis of the information contained in the passage.

Questions 1-3.

        It is common knowledge that ability to do a particular job and performance on the job do not always go hand in hand.   Persons with great potential abilities sometimes fall down on the job because of laziness or lack of interest in the job, while persons with mediocre talents have often achieved excellent results through their industry and their loyalty to the interests of their employers.   It is clear, therefore, that in a balanced personnel program, measures of employee ability need to be supplemented by measures of employee performance, for the final test of any employee is his performance on the job.

1.   The *MOST* accurate of the following statements, on the basis of the above   1._____
      paragraph, is that
            A.   employees who lack ability are usually not industrious
            B.   an employee's attitudes are more important than his abilities
            C.   mediocre employees who are interested in their work are preferable to
                  employees who possess great ability
            D.   superior capacity for performance should be supplemented with
                  proper attitudes

2.   On the basis of the above paragraph, the employee of most value to his   2._____
      employer is *NOT* necessarily the one who
            A.   best understands the significance of his duties
            B.   achieves excellent results
            C.   possesses the greatest talents
            D.   produces the greatest amount of work

3.   According to the above paragraph, an employee's efficiency is *BEST*   3._____
      determined by an
            A.   appraisal of his interest in his work
            B.   evaluation of the work performed by him
            C.   appraisal of his loyalty to his employer
            D.   evaluation of his potential ability to perform his work

Questions 4-5.

The cabinet shall be *fabricated* entirely of 22-gage stainless steel with #4 satin finish on all exposed surfaces. The face trim shall be one-piece construction with no mitres or welding, 1" wide and 1/4" to the wall. All doors shall be mounted on heavy-duty stainless steel piano hinges and have a concealed lock.

4. As used in the above paragraph, the word *fabricated* means, most nearly,   4._____
   A. made   B. designed   C. cut   D. plated

5. According to the above paragraph, a satin finish is to be used on surfaces   5._____
   A. to be welded   B. that are visible
   C. on which the hinges are mounted
   D. that are to be covered

Questions 6-10.

Many people still think accidents just happen – that they are due to bad luck. Nothing could be further from the truth.

Evidence of this is in the drop in accidents among employees of the City since the Safety Program started.

The one-out-of-a-hundred accidents that cannot be prevented might be called "Acts of God." They are things like lightning, earthquakes, tornadoes, and tidal waves that we are powerless to prevent – although we can take precautions against them which will cut down the accident rate.

The other ninety-nine percent of the accidents clearly have a man-made cause. If you trace back far enough, you'll find that some where, somehow, someone could have done something to prevent these accidents. For just about every accident, there is some fellow who fouled up. He didn't protect himself, he didn't use the right equipment, he wasn't alert, he lost his temper, he didn't have his mind on his work, he was "kidding around," or he took a shortcut because he was just too lazy.

We must all work together to improve safety and prevent injury and death.

6. The *one* of the following titles which *BEST* describes the subject matter of   6._____
   the above passage is:
   A. Acts of God
   B. The Importance of Safety Consciousness
   C. Safety in the City   D. Working Together

7. After the City began to operate a safety program, it was found that   7._____
   A. the number of accidents was reduced
   B. production decreased
   C. accidents stayed the same but employees were more careful
   D. the element of bad luck did not change

8. *One* cause of accidents that is *NOT* mentioned in the above passage is   8._____
   A. failure to keep alert   B. taking a short cut
   C. using the wrong equipment   D. working too fast

9. The number of accidents caused by such things as hurricanes can be   9._____
    A. changed only by an "Act of God"
    B. eliminated by strict adherence to safety rules
    C. increased by being too careful
    D. reduced by proper safety precautions

10. The percentage of accidents that occur as a result of things that cannot   10._____
be prevented is, approximately,
    A. 1 percent   B. 10 percent   C. 50 percent   D. 99 percent

Questions 11-15.

The most effective control mechanism to prevent gross incompetence on the part of public employees is a good personnel program. The personnel officer in the line departments and the central personnel agency should exert positive leadership to raise levels of performance. Although the key factor is the quality of the personnel recruited, staff members other than personnel officers can make important contributions to efficiency. Administrative analysts, now employed in many agencies, make detailed studies of organization and procedures, with the purpose of eliminating delays, waste, and other inefficiencies. Efficiency is, however, more than a question of good organization and procedures; it is also the product of the attitudes and values of the public employees. Personal motivation can provide the will to be efficient. The best management studies will not result in substantial improvement of the performance of those employees who feel no great urge to work up to their abilities.

11. The passage indicates that the *key* factor in preventing gross incompetence   11._____
of public employees is the
    A. hiring of administrative analysts to assist personnel people
    B. utilization of effective management studies
    C. overlapping of responsibility
    D. quality of the employees hired

12. According to the above passage, the central personnel agency staff should   12._____
    A. work more closely with administrative analysts in the line departments than with personnel officers
    B. make a serious effort to avoid jurisdictional conflicts with personnel officers in line departments
    C. contribute to improving the quality of work of public employees
    D. engage in a comprehensive program to change the public's negative image of public employees

13. The author of the passage believes that efficiency in an organization can   13._____
BEST be brought about by
    A. eliminating ineffective control mechanisms
    B. instituting sound organizational procedures
    C. promoting competent personnel
    D. recruiting people with desire to do good work

14. According to the passage, the purpose of administrative analysis in a public   14._____
    agency is to
    A. *prevent* injustice to the public employee
    B. *promote* the efficiency of the agency
    C. *protect* the interests of the public
    D. *ensure* the observance of procedural due process

15. The passage *implies* that a considerable rise in the quality of work of public   15._____
    employees can be brought about by
    A. encouraging positive employee attitudes toward work
    B. controlling personnel officers who exceed their powers
    C. creating warm personal associations among public employees in an
       agency
    D. closing loopholes in personnel organizations and procedures

Questions 16-25.   Answer questions 16 through 25 based on the following instructions:

INSTRUCTIONS FOR PREPARATION AND PLACEMENT OF RAT BAITS

a.   Fresh baits are the most acceptable to rats, so mix only enough bait for current
      needs.   Use a binder of molasses or of vegetable, mineral or fish oil in cereal or
      dry baits to hold the poison and the dry bait together and to aid in mixing.

b.   Mix an emetic, usually tartar emetic, with zinc phosphide and other more toxic
      bait formulations to protect animals other than rodents, even though
      acceptability of such baits to the rodents is thereby reduced.

c.   Mix bait as directed.   Too much poison may give the bait a strong taste or odor.
      Too little will not kill but may result in "bait shyness." Excessive amounts of
      poison increase the danger to man and to domestic animals.

d.   Mix baits well.   Poor mixing results in non-uniform baits and poor kills and
      speeds development of bait shyness.   Mechanical bait-mixing equipment is
      necessary where large quantities of bait are mixed routinely.

e.   Clearly label poisons and mixing equipment.   Do not use bait-mixing
      equipment for other purposes.   Lock up poisons and mixing equipment when
      not in use.   Treat all poisons with respect. Read and follow all label instructions.
      Avoid inhaling powders or getting poisons on hands, clothes, or utensils from
      which they may reach the mouth.   Wear rubber gloves when handling poisons.
      Always mix poisons in a well-ventilated place, particularly when mixing dry
      ingredients.

f.   If anti-coagulant baits are used, they should be placed in paper, metal, or plastic
      pie plates or in permanent bait stations.   Be liberal in baiting.   For
      anti-coagulants to be fully effective, repeated doses must be consumed by every
      rodent at a given location for a period of five or more consecutive days.

g.   Protect animals other than domestic rodents, and shield baits from the weather
      under shelter or with bait boxes, boards, pipes, or cans.

h.   Note locations of all bait containers so that inspections can be made rapidly and the bait that has been consumed can be quickly replaced.   (Bait consumption is generally heavy right after initial placement, making daily inspection and replacement advisable for the first 3 days after regular feeding begins.)

i.   At each inspection, smooth the surface of the baits so that new signs of feeding will show readily.   Replace moldy, wet, caked, or insect-infested baits with fresh ones.   If a bait remains undisturbed for several successive inspections, move it to an area showing fresh rodent signs.

j.   Use shallow bait containers fastened to the floor, or containers of sufficient weight to prevent the rodents from overturning them or dragging them to their burrows.   A roofing tack driven through metal or fiber containers into the floor reduces spillage.

k.   When single-dose poisons are used, wrap one-shot poison foot baits in 4" x 4" paper squares to form "torpedoes" about the size of a large olive.   These may be tossed readily into otherwise inaccessible places.   If several types of bait such as meat, fish, or cereal are to be distributed at the same time, a different color of paper should be used for each of the various types of bait.

l.   Be generous with baits.   Too few baits, or poorly-placed baits, may miss many rodents.   Bait liberally where signs of rat activity are numerous and recent.   In light or moderate infestations, torpedoes containing a single-dose poison, such as reds quill, have given good control when applied at a minimum rate of 20 baits per private residence.   As many as 100 to 200 baits may be required for premises with heavy rodent infestations .

m.   Place baits in hidden sites out of reach of children and pets.

n.   Inspect and rebait as needed, using another poison and another bait material when the rats become shy of the original baits.

16.   According to the above instructions, if you find, upon inspection, that your baits are overrun with insects, you should   16._____
     A.   replace the baits with fresh baits
     B.   move the baits to another station
     C.   add more rodenticide to the baits and re-mix them
     D.   apply the appropriate insecticide to the baits

17.   According to the above instructions, if you want to make sure you do *NOT* get poor kills, you should   17._____
     A.   mix large quantities of baits routinely
     B.   stick to one poison   C.   mix the baits well
     D.   use deep bait containers that cannot be easily overturned

18.   According to the above instructions, the equipment which is used for mixing bait should be   18._____
     A.   cleaned routinely   B.   mechanically easy to handle
     C.   easily disposable   D.   labeled clearly

Test 1

19. According to the above instructions, making the surface of the bait smooth   19._____
every time that you inspect the bait containers is
   A.   proper because it disturbs the insect infestation of the bait
   B.   improper because it will make the bait even less uniform if it was
        already mixed poorly
   C.   proper because it will help you determine if new signs of feeding are
        present
   D.   improper because it increases the presence of human odor on the bait
        and discourages rodents

20. According to the above instructions, if you are making a bait with zinc   20._____
phosphide, it is *MOST* important to
   A.   prepare a generous amount so you can bait liberally where signs of rat
        activity are numerous
   B.   use molasses to insure that the bait will be uniform
   C.   shield the bait from the weather
   D.   mix an emetic with the bait

21. According to the above instructions, you should substitute one poison for   21._____
another poison when the
   A.   bait consumption is heavy after initial placement
   B.   rodents become shy of the original baits
   C.   poison is dangerous to domestic animals
   D.   rodents are able to drag the baits to their burrows

22. According to the above instructions, when you handle poisons, you should   22._____
   A.   use mechanical bait-making equipment
   B.   wear rubber gloves
   C.   never place them in paper plates
   D.   always mix them with moist ingredients

23. According to the above instructions, if you plan to distribute several types   23._____
of bait at the same time in the form of "torpedoes," you should
   A.   select only anti-coagulant baits for this purpose
   B.   reduce the possibility of bait spillage by driving a roofing tack through
        the container into the floor
   C.   use a different color of paper for each of the various types of bait
   D.   make sure that the rodent does not consume repeated doses for more
        than a period of five consecutive days at the same location

24. According to the above instructions, mixing too much poison in the bait   24._____
   A.   may bring about bait shyness
   B.   permits you to make less frequent re-inspections
   C.   increases the danger to other life
   D.   may be necessary when anti-coagulants are used

25. According to the above instructions, if grain is to be used as bait,   25._____
   A.   rodents will not accept it if it is mixed with fish oil
   B.   you will only be able to make "torpedoes"
   C.   it will not be necessary to check the bait for fresh rodent signs
   D.   a binder should also be used to aid in mixing

94

TEST 2

Questions 1-4.

Cylindrical surfaces are the most common form of finished surfaces found on machine parts, although flat surfaces are also very common; hence, many metal-cutting processes are for the purpose of producing either cylindrical or flat surfaces. The machines used for cylindrical or flat shapes may be, and often are, utilized also for forming the various irregular or special shapes required on many machine parts. Because of the prevalence of cylindrical and flat surfaces, the student of manufacturing practice should learn first about the machines and methods employed to produce these surfaces. The cylindrical surfaces may be internal as in holes and cylinders. Any one part may, of course, have cylindrical sections of different diameters and lengths and include flat ends or shoulders and, frequently, there is a threaded part or possibly some finished surface that is not circular in cross-section. The prevalence of cylindrical surfaces on machine parts explains why lathes are found in all machine shops. It is important to understand the various uses of the lathe because many of the operations are the same fundamentally as those performed on other types of machine tools.

1. According to the above paragraph, the most common form of finished surfaces found on machine parts is
   A. cylindrical   B. elliptical   C. flat   D. square

   1._____

2. According to the above paragraph, any one part of cylindrical surfaces may Have
   A. chases   B. shoulders   C. keyways   D. splines

   2._____

3. According to the above paragraph, lathes are found in all machine shops because cylindrical surfaces on machine parts are
   A. scarce   B. internal   C. common   D. external

   3._____

4. As used in the above paragraph, the word *processes* means
   A. operations   B. purposes   C. devices   D. tools

   4._____

Questions 5-6.

The principle of interchangeability requires manufacture to such specification that component parts of a device may be selected at random and assembled to fit and operate satisfactorily. Interchangeable manufacture, therefore, requires that parts be made to definite limits of error, and to fit gages instead of mating parts. Interchangeability does not necessarily involve a high degree of precision; stove lids, for example, are interchangeable but are not particularly accurate, and carriage bolts and nuts are not precision products but are completely interchangeable. Interchangeability may be employed in unit-production as well as mass-production systems of manufacture.

5. According to the above paragraph, in order for parts to be interchangeable, they must be
   A. precision-machined   B. selectively-assembled
   C. mass-produced   D. made to fit gages

   5._____

6. According to the above paragraph, carriage bolts are interchangeable   6._____
    because they are
    A. precision-made   B. sized to specific tolerances
    C. individually matched products
    D. produced in small units

Questions 7-9.

The soda-acid fire extinguisher is the commonest type of water-solution extinguisher in which pressure is used to expel the water. The chemicals used are sodium bicarbonate (baking soda) and sulfuric acid. The sodium bicarbonate is dissolved in water, and this solution is the extinguishing agent. The extinguishing value of the stream is that of an equal quantity of water.

7. According to the above paragraph, the soda-acid extinguisher, compared to   7._____
    others of the same type, is the
    A. most widely used
    B. most effective in putting out fire
    C. cheapest to operate   D. easiest to operate

8. In the soda-acid extinguisher, the fire is put out by a solution of sodium   8._____
    bicardonate *and*
    A. sulfuric acid   B. baking soda
    C. soda-acid   D. water

9. According to the above paragraph, the sodium bicarbonate solution,   9._____
    compared to water, is
    A. more effective in putting out fires
    B. less effective in putting out fires
    C. equally effective in putting out fires
    D. more or less effective, depending upon the type of fire

Questions 10-12.

Some gases which may be inhaled have an irritant effect on the respiratory tract. Among them are ammonia fumes, hydrogen sulfide, nitrous fumes, and phosgene. Persons who have been exposed to irritant gases must lie down at once and keep absolutely quiet until the doctor arrives. The action of some of these gases may be delayed, and at first the fictim may show few or no symptoms.

10. According to the above paragraph, the part of the body that is most affected   10._____
    by irritant gases is the
    A. heart   B. lungs   C. skin   D. nerves

11. According to the above paragraph, a person who has inhaled an irritant   11._____
    gas should be
    A. given artificial respiration B. made to rest
    C. wrapped in blankets   D. made to breathe smelling salts

12. A person is believed to have come in contact with an irritant gas but he does   12._____
    not become sick immediately. According to the above paragraph, we may
    conclude that the person
    A. did not really come in contact with the gas
    B. will become sick later
    C. came in contact with a small amount of gas
    D. may possibly become sick later

Questions 13-17.

At one time people thought that in the interview designed primarily to obtain
information, the interviewer had to resort to clever and subtle lines of questioning in order
to accomplish his ends.   Some people still believe that this is necessary, but it is not so.
An example of the "tricky" approach may be seen in the work of a recent study.   The
study deals with materials likely to be buried beneath deep defenses.   Interviewers
utilized methods of questioning which, in effect, trapped the interviewee and destroyed
his defenses.   Doubtless, these methods succeeded in bringing out items of
information which straightforward questions would have missed.   Whether they missed
more information than they obtained and whether they obtained the most important facts,
must remain unanswered questions.   In defense of the "clever" approach, it is often said
that, in many situations, the interviewee is motivated to conceal information or to distort
what he chooses to report.

Technically, it is likely that a highly skilled interviewer can, given the time and the
inclination, penetrate the interviewee's defenses and get information which the latter
intended to keep hidden. It is unlikely that the interviewer could successfully elicit all of
the information that might be relevant.   If, for example, he found that an applicant for
financial assistance was heavily in debt to gamblers, he might not care about getting any
other information.   There are situations in which one item, if answered in the "wrong"
way, is enough. Ordinarily, this is not true.   The usual situation is that there are many
considerations and that the plus and minus features must be weighed before a decision
may be made.   It is therefore important to obtain complete information.

13. According to the above passage, it was generally believed that an interviewer   13._____
    would have difficulty in obtaining the information he sought from a person if he
    A. were tricky in his methods
    B. were open and frank in his approach
    C. were clever in his questioning
    D. utilized carefully prepared questions

14. The passage does NOT reveal whether the type of questions used   14._____
    A. trapped those being interviewed
    B. elicited facts which an open method of questioning might miss
    C. elicited the most important facts that were sought
    D. covered matters which those interviewed were reluctant to talk about
       openly

15. An argument in favor of the "tricky" or "clever" interviewing technique is that,   15._____
    unless this approach is used, the person interviewed will NOT
    A. offer to furnish all pertinent information
    B. answer questions concerning routine data
    C. clearly understand what is being sought
    D. want to continue the interview

16. According to the above passage, in favorable circumstances, a talented   16._____
interviewer would be able to obtain from the person interviewed information
    A. which the person regards as irrelevant
    B. which the person intends to conceal
    C. about the person's family background
    D. which the person would normally have forgotten

17. According to the above passage, a highly skilled interviewer should   17._____
concentrate, in most cases, on getting
    A. one outstanding fact about the interviewee which would do away with
        the need for prolonged questioning
    B. facts which the interviewee wanted to conceal because these would
        be the most relevant in making a decision
    C. all the facts so that he can consider their relative values before
        reaching any conclusion
    D. information about any bad habits of the interviewee, such as gambling,
        which would make further questioning unnecessary

Questions 18-22.

For a period of nearly fifteen years, beginning in the mid-1950's, higher
education sustained a phenomenal rate of growth. The factors principally responsible
were continuing improvement in the rate of college entrance by high school graduates, a
50-percent increase in the size of the college-age (eighteen to twenty-one) group, and –
until about 1967 – a rapid expansion of university research activity supported by the
federal government.

Today, as one looks ahead fifteen years to the year 2020, it is apparent that
each of these favorable stimuli will either be abated or turn into a negative factor. The
rate of growth of the college-age group has already diminished, and from 2010 to 2015
the size of the college-age group will shrink annually almost as fast as it grew from 1965
to 1970. From 2015 to 2020, this annual decrease will slow down so that by 2020 the
age-group will be about the same size as it was in 2019. This substantial net decrease
in the size of the college-age group over the next fifteen years will dramatically affect
college enrollments since, currently, 83 percent of undergraduates are twenty-one and
under, and another 11 percent are twenty-two to twenty-four.

18. Which one of the following factors is NOT mentioned in the above passage as   18._____
contributing to the high rate of growth of higher education?
    A. A large increase in the size of the eighteen to twenty-one age group
    B. The equalization of educational opportunities among socio-economic
        groups
    C. The federal budget impact on research and development spending in
        the higher education sector
    D. The increasing rate at which high-school graduates enter college

19. Based on the information in the above passage, the size of the college-age   19._____
group in 2020 will be
    A. larger than it was in 2019
    B. larger than it was in 2005
    C. smaller than it was in 2015
    D. about the same as it was in 2010

20. According to the above passage, the tremendous rate of growth of higher education started around
    A. 1950   B. 1955   C. 1960   D. 1965
    20._____

21. The percentage of undergraduates who are over age 25 is, most nearly,
    A. 6%   B. 8%   C. 11%   D. 17%
    21._____

22. Which one of the following conclusions can be substantiated by the information given in the above passage?   The
    A. college-age group will be about the same size in 2010 as it was in 1965
    B. annual decrease in the size of the college-age group from 2010 to 2015 will be about the same as the annual increase from 1965 to 1970
    C. overall decrease in the size of the college-age group from 2010 to 2015 will be followed by an overall increase in its size from 2015 to 2020
    D. size of the college-age group will decrease at a fairly constant rate from 2005 to 2020
    22._____

Questions 23-25.

A fire of undetermined origin started in the warehouse shed of a flour mill. Although there was some delay in notifying the fire department, they practically succeeded in bringing the fire under control when a series of dust explosions occurred which caused the fire to spread and the main building was destroyed.   The fire department's efforts were considerably handicapped because it was undermanned, and the water pressure in the vicinity was inadequate.

23. From the information contained in the above paragraph, it is *MOST* accurate to state that the cause of the fire was
    A. suspicious   B. unknown   C. accidental
    D. arson   E. spontaneous combustion
    23._____

24. In the fire described above, the *MOST* important cause of the fire spreading to the main building was the
    A. series of dust explosions
    B. delay in notifying the fire department
    C. inadequate water pressure   D. lack of manpower
    D. wooden construction of the building
    24._____

25. In the fire described above, the fire department's efforts were handicapped *CHIEFLY* by
    A. poor leadership   B. outdated apparatus
    C. uncooperative company employees
    D. insufficient water pressure   E. poorly trained men
    25._____

Questions 26-30.

Upon the death of a member or former member of the retirement system there shall be paid to his estate, or to the person he had nominated by written designation, his accumulated deductions.   In addition, if he is a member who is in city service, there shall be paid a sum consisting of: an amount equal to the compensation he earned while a member during the three months immediately preceding his death, or, if the total number of years of allowable service exceeds five there shall be paid an amount equal to the compensation he earned while a member during the six months immediately preceding his death; and the reserve-for-increased-take-home-pay, if any.

Payment for the expense of burial, not exceeding two hundred and fifty dollars, may be made to a relative or friend who, in the absence or failure of the designated beneficiary, assumes this responsibility.

Until the first retirement benefit payment has been made, where a member has not selected an option, the member will be considered to be in city service, and the death benefits provided above will be paid instead of the retirement allowance. The member, or upon his death, his designated beneficiary, may provide that the actuarial equivalent of the benefit otherwise payable in a lump sum shall be paid in the form of an annuity payable in installments; the amount of such annuity is determined at the time of the member's death on the basis of the age of the beneficiary at that time.

26. Suppose that a member who has applied for retirement benefits without selecting an option dies before receiving any payments. According to the information in the above passage, this member's beneficiary would be entitled to receive
    A. an annuity based on the member's age at the time of his death
    B. a death benefit only
    C. the member's retirement allowance only
    D. the member's retirement allowance, plus a death-benefit payment in a lump sum

26._____

27. Suppose that a member died on June 15, 2007, while still in city service. He Had joined the retirement system in March 1990. During the year preceding his death, he earned $75,000. Based on the information in the above passage, the designated beneficiary of this member would be entitled to receive all of the following *EXCEPT*
    A. a payment of $37,500
    B. payment of burial expense up to $250
    C. the member's accumulated deductions
    D. the reserve-for-increased-take-home-pay, if any

27._____

28. According to the information in the above passage, the amount of the benefit payable upon the death of a member is based, in part, on the
    A. length of city service during which the deceased person was a member
    B. number of beneficiaries the deceased member had nominated
    C. percent of the deceased member's deductions for social security
    D. type of retirement plan to which the deceased member belonged

28._____

29. According to the information in the above passage, which one of the following statements concerning the payment of death benefits is *CORRECT?*
    A. In order for a death benefit to be paid, the deceased member must have previously nominated, in writing, someone to receive the benefit
    B. Death benefits are paid upon the death of members who are in city service
    C. A death benefit must be paid in one lump sum
    D. When a retired person dies, his retirement allowance is replaced by a death-benefit payment

29._____

30. According to the information in the above passage, the   30._____
amount of annuity payments made to a beneficiary in monthly installments in lieu
of a lump-sum payment is determined by the
   A.   length of member's service at the time of his death
   B.   age of the beneficiary at the time of the member's death
   C.   member's age at retirement
   D.   member's age at the time of his death

_____

KEYS (CORRECT ANSWERS)

TEST 1					TEST 2			
1.	D	11.	D		1.	A	16.	B
2.	C	12.	C		2.	B	17.	C
3.	B	13.	D		3.	C	18.	B
4.	A	14.	B		4.	A	19.	C
5.	B	15.	A		5.	D	20.	B
6.	B	16.	A		6.	B	21.	A
7.	A	17.	C		7.	A	22.	B
8.	D	18.	D		8.	D	23.	B
9.	D	19.	C		9.	C	24.	A
10.	A	20.	D		10.	B	25.	D
		21	B		11.	B	26.	B
		22	B		12.	D	27.	B
		23.	C		13.	B	28.	A
		24.	C		14.	C	29.	B
		25.	D		15.	A	30.	B

_____

READING COMPREHENSION
UNDERSTANDING AND INTERPRETING WRITTEN MATERIAL

EXAMINATION SECTION
TEST 1

DIRECTIONS: Each question or incomplete statement is followed by several suggested answers or completions. Select the one that *BEST* answers the question or completes the statement. *PRINT THE LETTER OF THE CORRECT ANSWER IN THE SPACE AT THE RIGHT.*

Questions 1-7.

DIRECTIONS: All questions are to be answered *SOLELY* on the basis of the information contained in the passage

Snow-covered roads spell trouble for motorists all winter long. Clearing highways of snow and ice to keep millions of motor vehicles moving freely is a tremendous task. Highway departments now rely, to a great extent, on chemical de-icers to get the big job done. Sodium chloride, in the form of commercial salt, is the de-icer most frequently used.

There is no reliable evidence to prove that salt reduces highway accidents. But available statistics are impressive. For example, before Massachusetts used chemical de-icers, it had a yearly average of 21 fatal accidents and 1,635 injuries attributed to cars skidding on snow or ice. Beginning in 1990, the state began fighting hazardous driving *conditions with* chemical de-icers. During the period 1990-2000, there was a yearly average of only seven deaths and 736 injuries
as a result of skids.

Economical and effective in a moderately low temperature range, salt is increasingly popular with highway departments, but not so popular with individual car owners. Salty slush eats away at metal, including auto bodies. It also sprinkles windshields with a fine-grained spray which dries on contact, severely reducing visibility. However, drivers who are hindered or immobilized by heavy winter weather favor the liberal use of products such as sodium chloride. When snow blankets roads, these drivers feel that the quickest way to get back to the safety of driving on bare pavement is through use of de-icing salts.

1. The *MAIN* reason given by the above passage for the use of sodium chloride as a de-icer is that it
    A. has no harmful side effects
    B. is economical
    C. is popular among car owners
    D. reduces highway accidents

1._____

2. The above passage may *BEST* be described as a(n)   2._____
    A. argument against the use of sodium chloride as a de-icer
    B. discussion of some advantages and disadvantages of sodium
       chloride as a de-icer
    C. recommendation to use sodium chloride as a de-icer
    D. technical account of the uses and effects of sodium chloride as a
       de-icer

3. Based on the above passage, the use of salt on snow-covered roadways   3._____
will eventually
    A. decrease the efficiency of the automobile fuel
    B. cause tires to deteriorate
    C. damage the surface of the roadway
    D. cause holes in the sides of cars

4. The average number of persons killed yearly in Massachusetts in car   4._____
accidents caused by skidding on snow or ice, before chemical de-icers
were used there, was
    A. 9   B. 12   C. 21   D. 30

5. According to the passage, it would be advisable to use salt as a de-icer   5._____
when
    A. outdoor temperatures are somewhat below freezing
    B. residues on highway surfaces are deemed to be undesirable
    C. snow and ice have low absorbency characteristics
    D. the use of a substance is desired which dries on contact

6. As a result of using chemical de-icers, the number of injuries resulting from   6._____
skids in Massachusetts was reduced by about
    A. 35%   B. 45%   C. 55%   D. 65%

7. According to the above passage, driver visibility can be severely reduced   7._____
by
    A. sodium chloride deposits on the windshield
    B. glare from salt and snow crystals
    C. salt spray covering the front lights
    D. faulty windshield wipers

Questions 8-10.

    An employee should call the Fire Department for any fire except a small one in a
wastebasket. This kind of fire can be put out with a fire extinguisher. If the employee is
not sure about the size of the fire, he should not wait to find out how big it is. He should
call the Fire Department at once.
    Every employee should know what to do when a fire starts. He should know how to
use the fire-fighting tools in the building and how to call the Fire Department. He should
also know where the nearest fire alarm box is. But the most important thing for an
employee to do in case of fire is to avoid panic.

8. If there is a small fire in a wastebasket, an employee should
    A. call the Fire Department
    B. let it burn itself out
    C. open a window
    D. put it out with a fire extinguisher

                           8._____

9. In case of fire, the most important thing for an employee to do is to
    A. find out how big it is
    B. keep calm
    C. leave the building right away
    D. report to his boss

                           9._____

10. If a large fire starts while he is at work, an employee should *always FIRST*
    A. call the Fire Department
    B. notify the Housing Superintendent
    C. remove inflammables from the building
    D. use a fire extinguisher

                          10._____

Questions 11-12.

Those correction theorists who are in agreement with severe and rigid controls as a normal part of the correctional process are confronted with a contradiction; this is so because a responsibility which is consistent with freedom cannot be developed in a repressive atmosphere. They do not recognize this contradiction when they carry out their programs with dictatorial force and expect convicted criminals exposed to such programs to be reformed into free and responsible citizens.

11. According to the above paragraph, those correction theorists are faced with a contradiction who
    A. are in favor of the enforcement of strict controls in a prison
    B. believe that to develop a sense of responsibility, freedom must not be restricted
    C. take the position that the development of responsibility consistent with freedom is not possible in a repressive atmosphere
    D. think that freedom and responsibility can be developed only in a democratic atmosphere

                          11._____

12. According to the above paragraph, a repressive atmosphere in a prison
    A. does not conform to present-day ideas of freedom of the individual
    B. is admitted by correction theorists to be in conflict with the basic principles of the normal correctional process
    C. is advocated as the best method of maintaining discipline when rehabilitation is of secondary importance
    D. is not suitable for the development of a sense of responsibility consistent with freedom

                          12._____

Questions 13-16.

Abandoned cars – with tires gone, chrome stripped away, and windows smashed – have become a common sight on the City's streets. In 1990, more than 72,000 were deposited at curbs by owners who never came back, an increase of 15,000 from the year before and more than 30 times the number abandoned a decade ago. In January, 1991, the City's Environmental Protection Administrator asked the State Legislature to pass a law requiring a buyer of a new automobile to deposit $100 and an owner of an automobile at the time the law takes effect to deposit $50 with the State Department of Motor Vehicles. In return, they would be given a certificate of deposit which would be passed on to each succeeding owner. The final owner would get the deposit money back if he could present proof that he has disposed of his car "in an environmentally acceptable manner." The Legislature has given no indication that it plans to rush ahead on the matter.

13. The number of cars abandoned in City streets in 1980 was, most nearly,   13._____
    A. 2,500   B. 12,000   C. 27,500   D. 57,000

14. The proposed law would require a person who owned a car bought before   14._____
    the law was passed to deposit
        A. $100 with the State Department of Motor Vehicles
        B. $50 with the Environmental Protection Administration
        C. $100 with the State Legislature
        D. $50 with the State Department of Motor Vehicles

15. The proposed law would require the State to return the deposit money *only*   15._____
    when the
        A. original owner of the car shows proof that he sold it
        B. last owner of the car shows proof that he got rid of the car in a
           satisfactory way
        C. owner of the car shows proof that he has transferred the certificate
           of deposit to the next owner
        D. last owner of a car returns the certificate of deposit

16. The *main* idea or theme of the above article is that   16._____
        A. a proposed new law would make it necessary for car owners in the
           State to pay additional taxes
        B. the State Legislature is against a proposed law to require deposits
           from automobile owners to prevent them from abandoning their cars
        C. the City is trying to find a solution for the increasing number of cars
           abandoned on its streets
        D. to pay for the removal of abandoned cars, the City's Environmental
           Protection Administrator has asked the State to fine automobile
           owners who abandon their vehicles

Questions 17-19.

The German roach is the most common roach in houses in the United States. Adults are pale brown and about 1/2-inch long; both sexes have wings as long as the body, and can be distinguished from other roaches by the two dark stripes on the pronotum. The female carries its egg capsule protruding from her abdomen until the eggs are ready to hatch. This is the only common house-infesting species which carries the egg capsule for such an extended period of time. A female will usually produce 4 to 8 capsules in her lifetime. Each capsule contains 30 to 48 eggs which hatch out in about 28 days at ordinary room temperature. The completion of the nymphal stage under room conditions requires 40 to 125 days. German roaches may live as adults for as long as 303 days.

It is stated about that the German cockroach is the most commonly encountered of the house-infesting species in the United States. The reasons for this are somewhat complex, but the understanding of some of the factors involved are basic to the practice of pest control. In the first place, the German cockroach has a larger number of eggs per capsule and a shorter hatching time than do the other species. It also requires a shorter period from hatching until sexual maturity, so that within a given period of time a population of German roaches will produce a larger number of eggs. On the basis of this fact, we can state that this species has a high reproductive potential. Since the female carries the egg capsule during nearly the entire time that the embryos are developing within the egg, many hazards of the environment which may affect the eggs are avoided. This means that more nymphs are likely to hatch and that a larger portion of the reproductive potential is realized. The nymphs which hatch from each egg capsule tend to stay close to each other, and since they are often close to the female at time of hatching, there is a tendency for the population density to be high locally. Being smaller than most of the other roaches, they are able to conceal themselves in many places which are inaccessible to individuals of the larger species. All of these factors combined help to give the German cockroach an advantage with regard to group survival.

17. According to the above passage, the *most important* feature of the German roach which gives it an advantage over other roaches is its   17._____
    A. distinctive markings   B. immunity to disease
    C. long life span   D. power to reproduce

18. An *important* difference between an adult female German roach and an adult female of other species is the   18._____
    A. black bars or stripes which appear on the abdomen of the German roach
    B. German roach's preference for warm, moist places in which to breed
    C. long period of time during which the German roach carries the egg capsule
    D. presence of longer wings on the female German roach

19. A storeroom in a certain housing project has an infestation of German roaches, which includes 125 adult female. If the infestation is not treated and ordinary room temperature is maintained in the storeroom, *how many* eggs will hatch out during the lifetime of these females if they each lay 8 capsules containing 48 eggs each?   19._____
    A. 1,500   B. 48,000   C. 96,000   D. 303,000

Questions 20-22.

City governments have long had building codes which set minimum standards for building and for human occupancy. The code (or series of codes) makes provisions for standards of lighting and ventilation, sanitation, fire prevention, and protection. As a result of demands from manufacturers, builders, real estate people, tenement owners, and building-trades unions, these codes often have established minimum standards well below those that the contemporary society would accept as a rock-bottom minimum. Codes often become outdated, so that meager standards in one era become seriously inadequate a few decades later as society's concept of a minimum standard of living changes. Out-of-date codes, when still in use, have sometimes prevented the introduction of new devices and modern building techniques. Thus, it is extremely important that building codes keep pace with changes in the accepted concept of a minimum standard of living.

20. According to the above passage, all of the following considerations in building planning would probably be covered in a building code *EXCEPT*
    A. closet space as a percentage of total floor area
    B. size and number of windows required for rooms of differing sizes
    C. placement of fire escapes in each line of apartments
    D. type of garbage disposal units to be installed

20._____

21. According to the above passage, if an ideal building code were to be created, how would the established minimum standards in it compare to the ones that are presently set by city governments? They would
    A. *be lower* than they are at present
    B. *be higher* than they are at present
    C. *be comparable* to the present minimum standards
    D. *vary* according to the economic group that sets them

21._____

22. On the basis of the above passage, *what* is the reason for difficulties in introducing new building techniques?
    A. Builders prefer techniques which represent the rock-bottom minimum desired by society.
    B. Certain manufacturers have obtained patents on various building methods to the exclusion of new techniques.
    C. The government does not want to invest money in techniques that will soon be outdated.
    D. New techniques are not provided for in building codes which are not up to date.

22._____

Questions 23-25.

A flameproof fabric is defined as one which, when exposed to small sources of ignition such as sparks or smoldering cigarettes, does not burn beyond the vicinity of the source of the ignition. Cotton fabrics are the materials commonly used that are considered most hazardous. Other materials, such as acetate rayons and linens, are somewhat less hazardous, and woolens and some natural silk fabrics, even when untreated, are about the equal of the average treated cotton fabric insofar as flame spread and ease of ignition are concerned. The method of application is to immerse the fabric in a flameproofing solution. The container used must be large enough so that all the fabric is thoroughly wet and there are no folds which the solution does not penetrate.

23. According to the above paragraph, a flameproof fabric is one which   23._____
    A. is unaffected by heat and smoke
    B. resists the spread of flames when ignited
    C. burns with a cold flame
    D. cannot be ignited by sparks or cigarettes
    E. may smolder but cannot burn

24. According to the above paragraph, woolen fabrics which have not been   24._____
flameproofed are as likely to catch fire as
    A. treated silk fabrics
    B. treated acetate rayon fabrics
    C. untreated linen fabrics
    D. untreated synthetic fabrics
    E. treated cotton fabrics

25. In the method described above, the flameproofing solution is *BEST* applied   25._____
to the fabric by
    A. sponging the fabric   B. spraying the fabric
    C. dipping the fabric   D. brushing the fabric
    E. sprinkling the fabric

———

KEY (CORRECT ANSWERS)

1.	B		11.	A
2.	B		12.	D
3.	D		13.	A
4.	C		14.	D
5.	A		15.	B
6.	C		16.	C
7.	A		17.	D
8.	D		18.	C
9.	B		19.	B
10.	A		20.	A

21.	B
22.	D
23.	B
24.	E
25.	C

TEST 2

DIRECTIONS FOR THIS SECTION:

All questions are to be answered *SOLELY* on the basis of the information contained in the passage.

Each question or incomplete statement is followed by several suggested answers or completions. Select the one that *BEST* answers the question or completes the statement. *PRINT THE LETTER OF THE CORRECT ANSWER IN THE SPACE AT THE RIGHT.*

Questions 1-4.

Safety belts provide protection for the passengers of a vehicle by preventing them from crashing around inside if the vehicle is involved in a collision. They operate on the principle similar to that used in the packaging of fragile items. You become a part of the vehicle package and you are kept from being tossed about inside if the vehicle is suddenly decelerated. Many injury-causing collisions at low speeds – for example, at city intersections – could have been injury-free if the occupants had fastened their safety belts. There is a double advantage to the driver in that it not only protects him from harm, but prevents him from being yanked away from the wheel, thereby permitting him to maintain control of the car. Since, without seat belts, the risk of injury is about 50% greater, and the risk of death is about 30% greater, the State Vehicle and Traffic Law provided that a motor vehicle manufactured or assembled after June 30, 1964 and designated as a 1965 or later model should have two safety belts for the front seat. It also provides that a motor vehicle manufactured after June 30, 1966 and designated as a 1967 or later model should have at least one safety belt for the rear seat for each passenger for which the rear seat of such vehicle was designed.

1. The principle on which seat belts work is that
   A. a car and its driver and passengers are fragile
   B. a person fastened to the car will not be thrown around when the car slows down suddenly
   C. the driver and passengers of a car that is suddenly decelerated will be thrown forward
   D. the driver and passengers of an automobile should be packaged the way fragile items are packaged

   1._____

2. We can assume from the above passage that safety belts should be worn at all times because you can never tell when
   A. a car will be forced to turn off onto another road
   B. it will be necessary to shift into low gear to go up a hill
   C. you will have to speed up to pass another car
   D. a car may have to come to a sudden stop

   2._____

3. Besides preventing injury, an *additional* benefit from the use of safety belts is that
   A. collisions are fewer
   B. damage to the car is kept down
   C. the car can be kept under control
   D. the number of accidents at city intersections is reduced

   3._____

4. The risk of death in car accidents for people who don't use safety belts is   4._____
    A. 30% greater than the risk of injury
    B. 30% greater than for those who do use them
    C. 50% less than the risk of injury
    D. 50% greater than for those who use them

Questions 5-9.

Any person who is living in New York City and is otherwise eligible may be granted public assistance whether or not he has New York State residence. However, since New York City does not contribute to the cost of assistance granted to persons who are without State residence, the cases of all recipients must be formally identified as to whether or not each member of the household has State residence.

To acquire State residence a person must have resided in New York State continuously for one year. Such residence is not lost unless the person is out of the State continuously for a period of one year or longer. Continuous residence does not include any period during which the individual is a patient in a hospital, an inmate of a public institution or of an incorporated private institution, a resident on a military reservation, or a minor residing in a boarding home while under the care of an authorized agency. Receipt of public assistance does not prevent a person from acquiring State residence. State residence, once acquired, is not lost because of absence from the State while a person is serving in the U. S. Armed Forces or the Merchant Marine; nor does a member of the family of such a person lose State residence while living with or near that person in these circumstances.

Each person, regardless of age, acquires or loses State residence as an individual. There is no derivative State residence except for an infant at the time of birth. He is deemed to have State residence if he is in the custody of both parents and either one of them has State residence, or if the parent having custody of him has State residence.

5. According to the above passage, an infant is deemed to have New York   5._____
    State residence at the time of his birth if
    A. he is born in New York State but neither of his parents is a resident
    B. he is in the custody of only one parent, who is not a resident, but his other parent is a resident
    C. his brother and sister are residents
    D. he is in the custody of both his parents but only one of them is a resident

6. The Jones family consists of five members. Jack and Mary Jones have   6._____
    lived in New York State continuously for the past eighteen months after having lived in Ohio since they were born. Of their three children, one was born ten months ago and has been in the custody of his parents since birth. Their second child lived in Ohio until six months ago and then moved in with his parents. Their third child had never lived in New York until he moved with his parents to New York eighteen months ago. However, he entered the armed forces one month later and has not lived in New York since that time.
    Based on the above passage, how many members of the Jones family are New York State residents?
    A. 2   B. 3   C. 4   D. 5

7. Assuming that each of the following individuals has lived continuously in New York State for the past year, and has never previously lived in the State, *which one* of them is a New York State resident?
   A. Jack Salinas, who has been an inmate in a State correctional facility for six months of the year
   B. Fran Johnson, who has lived on an Army base for the entire year
   C. Arlene Snyder, who married a non-resident during the past year
   D. Gary Phillips, who was a patient in a Veterans Administration hospital for the entire year

7._____

8. The above passage implies that the reason for determining whether or not a recipient of public assistance is a State resident is that
   A. the cost of assistance for non-residents is not a New York City responsibility
   B. non-residents living in New York City are not eligible for public assistance
   C. recipients of public assistance are barred from acquiring State residence
   D. New York City is responsible for the full cost of assistance to recipients who are residents

8._____

9. Assume that the Rollins household in New York City consists of six members at the present time – Anne Rollins, her three children, her aunt, and her uncle. Anne Rollins and one of her children moved to New York City seven months ago. Neither of them had previously lived in New York State. Her other two children have lived in New York City continuously for the past two years, as has her aunt. Anne Rollins' uncle had lived in New York City continuously for many years until two years ago. He then entered the armed forces and has returned to New York City within the past month. Based on the above passage, how many members of the Rollins' household are New York State residents?
   A. 2   B. 3   C. 4   D. 6

9._____

Questions 10-12.

   The agreement under which a tenant rents property from a landlord is known as a lease. Generally speaking, leases are classified as either short-term or long-term in duration. They are further subdivided according to the method used to determine the amount of periodic rent payments. Of the many types of lease in use, the more commonly used ones are the following:
1. The straight or fixed lease is one in which rent may be paid in equal amounts throughout the duration of the lease. These are usually restricted to short-term leasing, or somewhat longer-term if clauses in the lease provide for periodic escalation of payments as the economy shifts.
2. Percentage leasing, used for short-term commercial leasing, provides the landlord with a stipulated percentage of a tenant's gross sales from goods and services sold on the premises, in addition to a fixed amount of rent.
3. The net lease, generally long-term (ten years or more), requires the tenant to pay all operating costs, including real estate taxes and insurance. In a net-net lease, the tenant further agrees to meet mortgage interest and principal payments.

4. An escalated lease, which is a long-term lease, requires rent to be of a stipulated base amount which periodically is subject to escalation in accordance with cost-of-living index scales, or in direct proportion to taxes, insurance, and operating costs.

10. Based on the information given in the passage, *which* type of lease is *most likely* to be advantageous to a landlord if there is a high rate of inflation?   10._____
   A. fixed lease
   B. percentage lease
   C. net lease
   D. escalated lease

11. On the basis of the above passage, *which* types of lease would generally be *MOST* suitable for a well-established textile company which requires permanent facilities for its large operations?   11._____
   A. Percentage lease and escalated lease
   B. Escalated lease and net lease
   C. Straight lease and net lease
   D. Straight lease and percentage lease

12. According to the above passage, the *only* type of lease which assures the same amount of rent throughout a specified interval is the   12._____
   A. straight lease
   B. percentage lease
   C. net-net lease
   D. escalated lease

Questions 13-18.

Basic to every office is the need for proper lighting. Inadequate lighting is a familiar cause of fatigue and serves to create a somewhat dismal atmosphere in the office. One requirement of proper lighting is that it be of an appropriate intensity. Intensity is measured in foot-candles. According to the Illuminating Engineering Society of New York, for casual seeing tasks such as in reception rooms, inactive file rooms, and other service areas, it is recommended that the amount of light be 30 foot-candles. For ordinary seeing tasks such as reading and work in active file rooms and in mail rooms, the recommended lighting is 100 foot-candles. For very difficult seeing tasks such as accounting, transcribing, and business-machine use, the recommended lighting is 150 foot-candles.

Lighting intensity is only one requirement. Shadows and glare are to be avoided. For example, the larger the proportion of a ceiling filled with lighting units, the more glare-free and comfortable the lighting will be. Natural lighting from windows is not too dependable because on dark wintry days windows yield little usable light, and on sunny, summer afternoons the glare from windows may be very distracting. Desks should not face the windows. Finally, the main lighting source ought to be overhead and to the left of the user.

13. According to the above passage, insufficient light in the office may cause   13._____
   A. glare   B. shadows   C. tiredness   D. distraction

14. Based on the above passage, *which* of the following must be considered when planning lighting arrangements? The   14._____
   A. amount of natural light present
   B. amount of work to be done
   C. level of difficulty of work to be done
   D. type of activity to be carried out

15. It can be inferred from the above passage that a well-coordinated lighting   15._____
scheme is likely to result in
  A. greater employee productivity
  B. elimination of light reflection
  C. lower lighting cost
  D. more use of natural light

16. Of the following, the *BEST* title for the above passage is: 16._____
  A. Characteristics of Light
  B. Light Measurement Devices
  C. Factors to Consider When Planning Lighting Systems
  D. Comfort vs. Cost When Devising Lighting Arrangements

17. According to the above passage, a foot-candle is a measurement of the   17._____
  A. number of bulbs used
  B. strength of the light
  C. contrast between glare and shadow
  D. proportion of the ceiling filled with lighting units

18. According to the above passage, the number of foot-candles of light that   18._____
would be needed to copy figures onto a payroll is
  A. less than 30 foot-candles   B. 30 foot-candles
  C. 100 foot-candles   D. 150 foot-candles

Questions 19-22.

A summons is an official statement ordering a person to appear in court. In traffic violation situations, summonses are used when arrests need not be made. The main reason for traffic summonses is to deter motorists from repeating the same traffic violation. Occasionally, motorists may make unintentional driving errors and sometimes they are unaware of correct driving regulations. In cases such as these, the policy should be to have the Officer verbally inform the motorist of the violation and warn him against repeating it. The purpose of this practice is not to limit the number of summonses, but rather to prevent the issuing of summonses when the violation is not due to deliberate intent or to inexcusable negligence.

19. According to the above passage, the *PRINCIPAL* reason for issuing traffic   19._____
summonses is to
  A. discourage motorists from violating these laws again
  B. increase the money collected by the city
  C. put traffic violators in prison
  D. have them serve as substitutes for police officers

20. The reason a verbal warning may sometimes be substituted for a summons   20._____
is to
  A. limit the number of summonses
  B. distinguish between excusable and inexcusable violations
  C. provide harsher penalties for deliberate intent than for inexcusable
     negligence
  D. decrease the caseload in the courts

115

21. The author of the above passage feels that someone who violated a traffic regulation because he did *not* know about the regulation should be
    A. put under arrest
    B. fined less money
    C. given a summons
    D. told not to do it again
    21._____

22. Using the distinctions made by the author of the above passage, the *one* of the following motorists to whom it would be *MOST* desirable to issue a summons is the one who exceeded the speed limit because he
    A. did not know the speed limit
    B. was late for an important business appointment
    C. speeded to avoid being hit by another car
    D. had a speedometer which was not working properly
    22._____

Questions 23-25.

Physical design plays a very significant role in crime rate. Crime rate has been found to increase almost proportionately with building height. The average number of crimes is much greater in higher buildings than in lower ones (equal to or less than six stories). What is most interesting is that in buildings of six stories or less, the project size or total number of units does not make a difference. It seems that, although larger projects encourage crime by fostering feelings of anonymity, isolation, irresponsibility, and lack of identity with surroundings, evidence indicates that larger projects encompassed in low buildings seem to offset what we may assume to be factors conducive to high crime rates. High-rise projects not only experience a higher rate of crime within the buildings, but a greater proportion of the crime occurs in the interior public spaces of these buildings as compared with those of the lower buildings. Lower buildings have more limited public space than higher ones. A criminal probably perceives that the interior public areas of buildings are where his victims are most vulnerable and where the possibility of his being seen or apprehended is minimal. Placement of elevators, entrance lobbies, fire stairs and secondary exits all are factors related to the likelihood of crimes taking place in buildings. The study of all of these elements should bear some weight in the planning of new projects.

23. According to the passage, *which* of the following *BEST* describes the relationship between building size and crime?
    A. Larger projects lead to a greater crime rate
    B. Higher buildings tend to increase the crime rate
    C. The smaller the number of project apartments in low buildings the higher the crime rate
    D. Anonymity and isolation serve to lower the crime rate in small buildings
    23._____

24. According to the passage, the likelihood of a criminal attempting a mugging in the interior public portions of a high-rise building is good because
    A. tenants will be constantly flowing in and out of the area
    B. there is easy access to fire stairs and secondary exits
    C. there is a good chance that no one will see him
    D. tenants may not recognize the victims of crime as their neighbors
    24._____

25. *Which* of the following is *implied* by the passage as an explanation for the
    fact that the crime rate is lower in large low-rise housing projects than in
    large high-rise projects?

    A. Tenants know each other better and take a greater interest in what
       happens in the project
    B. There is more public space where tenants are likely to gather
       together
    C. The total number of units in a low-rise project is fewer than the total
       number of units in a high-rise project
    D. Elevators in low-rise buildings travel quickly, thus limiting the
       amount of time in which a criminal can act

25. _____

KEY (CORRECT ANSWERS)

1.	B	11.	B
2.	D	12.	A
3.	C	13.	C
4.	B	14.	D
5.	D	15.	A
6.	B	16.	C
7.	C	17.	B
8.	A	18.	D
9.	C	19.	A
10.	D	20.	B

21.	D
22.	B
23.	B
24.	C
26.	A

READING COMPREHENSION
UNDERSTANDING AND INTERPRETING WRITTEN MATERIAL
EXAMINATION SECTION
TEST 1

DIRECTIONS: Each question or incomplete statement is followed by several suggested answers or completions. Select the one that BEST answers the question or completes the statement. *PRINT THE LETTER OF THE CORRECT ANSWER IN THE SPACE AT THE RIGHT.*

Questions 1-3.

DIRECTIONS: Questions 1 through 3 are to be answered SOLELY on the basis of the following paragraph.

Accident proneness is a subject which deserves much more objective and competent study than it has received to date. In discussing accident proneness, it is important to differentiate between the employee who is a *repeater* and one who is truly accident-prone. It is obvious that any person put on work of which he knows little without thorough training in safe practice for the work in question will be liable to injury until he does learn the *how* of it. Few workmen left to their own devices will develop adequate safe practices. Therefore, they must be trained. Only those who fail to respond to proper training should be regarded as accident-prone. The repeater whose accident record can be explained by a correctible physical defect, by correctible plant or machine hazards, by assignment to work for which he is not suited because of physical deficiencies or special abilities, cannot be fairly called *accident prone*.

1. According to the above paragraph, a person is considered accident prone if   1.____

    A.   he has accidents regardless of the fact that he has been properly trained
    B.   he has many accidents
    C.   it is possible for him to have accidents
    D.   he works at a job where accidents are possible

2. According to the above paragraph,   2.____

    A.   workers will learn the safe way of doing things if left to their own intelligence
    B.   most workers must be trained to be safe
    C.   a worker who has had more than one accident has not been properly trained
    D.   intelligent workers are always safe

3. According to the above paragraph, a person would not be called accident prone if the   3.____
cause of his accident was

    A.   a lack of interest in the job
    B.   recklessness
    C.   a low level of intelligence
    D.   eyeglasses that don't fit properly

Questions 4-9.

DIRECTIONS: Each question consists of a statement. You are to indicate whether the statement is TRUE (T) or FALSE (F). Questions 4 through 9 are to be answered
SOLELY on the basis of the following passage;

Every accident should be reported even though the accident seems very unimportant.
The man involved may be unharmed, yet it is necessary in the case of all accidents to forward
a written report containing all the facts that show how the accident occurred, including the
time and place. The reason for this action is that a situation which does not cause injury at
one time may cause serious injury at another time. A written report informs the safety director
of a dangerous condition and helps his investigation by supplying important facts. He can,
therefore, take steps to eliminate the hazard,

4. Only serious accidents should be reported.

5. If the man involved in an accident is unharmed, it is not necessary to send through a
    report.

6. An accident report should show how the accident happened and include the time and
    place of the accident.

7. A situation which does not cause an injury at one time cannot cause serious injury at
    another time.

8. When a written report of an accident is made, it means that the safety director is
    informed of a dangerous condition.

9. The facts in an accident report do not help the safety director in his investigation of the
    accident.

Questions 10-17.

DIRECTIONS: Each question consists of a statement. You are to indicate whether the statement is TRUE (T) or FALSE (F). Questions 10 through 17 are to be answered
SOLELY on the basis of the following passage.

The Mayor is in charge of the city government. He has his office in City Hall in downtown.
There are city rules, or laws, that all citizens must obey. For example, there is a law that no
one can throw things on the sidewalks or into the streets. We want our city to be clean and
beautiful. There are also traffic laws for the automobiles that use our city streets. For instance,
the cars cannot go at more than a certain speed. The drivers must stop when the traffic lights
turn red.

If people do not obey these rules or city laws, a policeman may arrest them. These laws
were made to protect other people who want to use the streets too.

10. The head of the city government is the Mayor.

11. The Mayor's office is in the Municipal Building.

12. The Mayor does not have to obey the city laws or rules.   12._____

13. Anyone who throws things on the sidewalks is breaking the law.   13._____

14. There is a traffic law that does not allow a car to go faster than a certain speed.   14._____

15. A driver does not have to stop when the traffic lights turn red.   15._____

16. A policeman may arrest a driver who does not obey the traffic laws.   16._____

17. People who use the streets are not protected by the traffic laws.   17._____

Questions 18-25.

DIRECTIONS: Each question consists of a statement. You are to indicate whether the state-
               ment is TRUE (T) or FALSE (F). Questions 18 through 25 are to be answered
               SOLELY on the basis of the following passage.

NEW YORK CITY

The name of New York City, as it appears on all official documents, is *The City of New York*. This name applies to all five boroughs which consolidated in 1898 to form what is known as Greater New York. The five boroughs are Manhattan, The Bronx, Brooklyn, Queens, and Richmond. The term Greater New York is seldom used at the present time, and often the city is called New York City to distinguish it from New York State. The two Boroughs of Brooklyn and Queens are located on Long Island and the Borough of Richmond is located on Staten Island. The Borough of Manhattan is located on Manhattan Island, while The Bronx is located on the mainland of New York State. Because the city is large, covers much territory, and has so many people, the United States Post Office has divided the city for its own convenience; therefore, the post office address of people living in Manhattan is New York, New York. For those living in the Borough of Brooklyn, the post office address is Brooklyn, New York; and, likewise, each borough has its own special post office address.

18. New York City is referred to on all official documents as *Greater New York City*.   18._____

19. The boroughs of New York City were joined together in 1898 to make up Greater New   19._____
    York.

20. Greater New York is made up of five boroughs.   20._____

21. The boroughs which make up New York City are   21._____
    The Bronx, Richmond, Brooklyn, Queens, and Nassau.

22. The borough of Queens is located on the mainland of New York State.   22._____

23. The Bronx and Brooklyn are part of Long Island.   23._____

24. A letter for Manhattan should be addressed to New York, New York.   24._____

25. Because New York City is so big, the Post Office has divided it into five different post   25._____
    office addresses.

KEY (CORRECT ANSWERS)

1.	A		11.	F
2.	B		12.	F
3.	D		13.	T
4.	F		14.	T
5.	F		15.	F
6.	T		16.	T
7.	F		17.	F
8.	T		18.	F
9.	F		19.	T
10.	T		20.	T

21.	F
22.	F
23.	F
24.	T
25.	T

———

TEST 2

Questions 1-4.

DIRECTIONS: Questions 1 through 4 are to be answered SOLELY on the basis of the following passage.

In the long run, a government will always encroach upon freedom to the extent which it has the power to do so; this is almost a natural law of politics since, whatever the intentions of the men who exercise political power, the sheer momentum of government leads to a constant pressure upon the liberties of the citizen. But in many countries, society has responded by throwing up its own defenses in the shape of social classes or organized corporations which, enjoying economic power and popular support, have been able to set limits to the scope of action of the executive. Such, for example, in England was the origin of all our liberties-won from government by the stand first of the feudal nobility, then of churches and political parties, and latterly of trade unions, commercial organizations, and the societies for promoting various causes. Even European lands which were arbitrarily ruled by the powers of the monarchy, though absolute in theory, were in their exercise checked in a similar fashion. Indeed, the fascist dictatorships of today are the first truly tyrannical governments which western Europe has known for centuries, and they have been rendered possible only because on coming to power they destroyed all forms of social organization which were in any way rivals to the state.

1. The MAIN idea of the above passage is BEST expressed as   1.____

    A. limited powers of monarchies
    B. the ideal of liberal government
    C. functions of trade unions
    D. ruthless ways of dictators

2. The writer maintains that there is a natural tendency for governments to   2.____

    A. become more democratic
    B. become fascist
    C. increase individual liberties
    D. assume more power

3. Monarchy was FIRST checked in England by the   3.____

    A. trade unions   B. church
    C. people   D. nobles

4. Fascist dictatorships differ from monarchies of recent times in   4.____

    A. getting things done by sheer momentum
    B. promoting various causes
    C. exerting constant pressure on liberties
    D. destroying people's organizations

Questions 5-8.

DIRECTIONS: Questions 5 through 8 are to be answered SOLELY on the basis of the following paragraph.

Very early on a summer's morning, the nicest thing to look at is a beach, before the
swimmers arrive. Usually all the litter has been picked up from the sand by the Park Department clean-up crew. Everything is quiet. All you can hear are the waves breaking and the sea
gulls calling to each other. The beach opens to the public at 10 A.M. Long before that time;
however, long lines of eager men, women, and children have driven up to the entrance. They
form long lines that wind around the beach waiting for the signal to move.

5. According to the above paragraph, before 10 A.M., long lines are formed that are made   5.
up of

A. cars   B. clean-up crews
C. men, women, and children   D. Park Department trucks

6. The season referred to in the above paragraph is   6.

A. fall   B. summer
C. winter   D. spring

7. The place the above paragraph is describing is a   7.

A. beach   B. Park
C. golf course   D. tennis court

8. According to the above paragraph, one of the things you notice early in the morning is   8
that

A. radios are playing   B. swimmers are there
C. the sand is dirty   D. the litter is gone

Questions 9-10.

DIRECTIONS: Questions 9 and 10 are to be answered SOLELY on the basis of the following
passage.

There have been almost as many definitions of *opinion* as there have been students of
the problem, and the definitions have ranged from such a statement as *inconsistent views
capable of being accepted by rational minds as true* to the *overt manifestation of an attitude.*
There are, however, a number of clearly outstanding factors among the various definitions
which form the sum total of the concept. Opinion is the stronghold of the individual. No *group*
ever had an opinion, and there is no mechanism except that of the individual mind capable of
forming an opinion. It is true, of course, that opinions can be altered or even created by the
stimuli of environment. In the midst of individual diversity and confusion, every question as it
rises into importance is subjected to a process of consolidation and clarification until there
emerge certain views, each held and advocated in common by bodies of citizens. When a
group of people accepts the same opinion, that opinion is public with respect to the group
accepting it. When there is not unanimous opinion, there is not one public but two or more.

9. On the basis of the above passage, it may be INFERRED that   9.____

   A. all individual opinions are subjected to consolidation by the influence of environ-
      mental stimuli
   B. governments are influenced by opinions held in common by large groups of citi-
      zens
   C. some of the elements of the extremely varied definitions of *opinion* are compatible
   D. when there is no unanimity, there is no public opinion

10. On the basis of the above passage, the MOST accurate of the following statement is: 10.____

   A. One definition of *opinion* implies that most individuals can accept inconsistent
      views on the same question
   B. One other definition of *opinion* implies that the individual's attitude concerning a
      question must be openly expressed before it can be considered as an opinion
   C. The individual opinion plays no part in the stand taken on a given question by a
      group after the individual has identified himself with the group
   D. There are no group opinions formed on relatively unimportant issues because of
      individual confusion

Questions 11-13.

DIRECTIONS: Questions 11 through 13 are to be answered SOLELY on the basis of the fol-
              lowing passage.

The word *propaganda* has fallen on evil days. As far as popular usage is concerned, its
reputation by now is probably lost irretrievably, for its connotation is almost invariably sinister
or evil. This is a pity for, in the struggle for men's minds, it is a weapon of great potential value.
Indeed, in the race against time that we are running, its constructive use is indispensable.
The student of propaganda must know that it is a term honorable in origin.

Propaganda is *good* or *bad* according to the virtue of the end to which it seeks to persuade us, and the methods it employs. Bad propaganda is distinguished by a disregard for
the welfare of those at whom it is directed. Such disregard either derives from, or eventually
results in, a lack of proper reverence for individuality, for the private person and our relation to
him. For *man* is substituted mass, and the *mass* is manipulated for selfish purposes. The
authoritarian reformist who believes he is acting *in the interest* of the masses is also involved
in this same disregard for personal integrity. Its final outcome is always the same-a disregard
for the individual. Good propaganda involves the deliberate avoidance of all casuistry. In so
far as good propaganda operates upon us at a level of our weakness or disability, its intent
must be to contribute a cure, not a sedative; inspiration, not an opiate; enlightenment, not
accentuation of our ignorance.

11. Of the following, the MOST suitable title for the above passage is   11.____

   A. PROPAGANDA AND SOCIETY
   B. PROPAGANDA FOR THE MASSES
   C. THE PROPER MEANING OF PROPAGANDA
   D. SES AND MISUSES OF PROPAGANDA

12. On the basis of the above passage, it may be INFERRED that 12.___

   A. some propaganda may employ unscrupulous methods to persuade us to ends that are justified
   B. the definition of the word *propaganda* has been changed
   C. the method of frequent repetition is an example of bad propaganda.
   D. the opportunity for the individual to challenge propaganda has decreased

13. On the basis of the above passage, it may be INFERRED that 13.___

   A. a reformer who believes in his cause should not employ propaganda to advance it
   B. good propaganda should be limited to operating against the levels of weakness of the individual
   C. propaganda may lose sight of the welfare of the individual in its appeal to the masses
   D. those who have privileged access to the media of mass communication must always accept high standards in their use of propaganda

Questions 14-15.

DIRECTIONS: Questions 14 and 15 are to be answered SOLELY on the basis of the following passage.

A steadfast concert for peace can never be maintained except by a partnership of democratic nations. No autocratic government could be trusted to keep faith within it or observe its covenants. It must be a league of honor, a partnership of opinion. Intrigue would eat its vitals away; the plotting of inner circles who could plan what they would, and render account to no one, would be a corruption seated at its very heart. Only free people can hold their purpose and their honor steady to a common end, and prefer the interests of mankind to any narrow interest of their own.

14. According to the above paragraph, only democratic nations can 14.___

   A. be free of plotting, intrigue, and corruption
   B. be trusted to do what is right and honorable
   C. plan programs which promote the interests of their country
   D. subordinate their own interests to those which benefit the entire world

15. It may be implied from the above passage that an autocratic government could NOT be trusted to respect its international agreements because it 15.___

   A. exemplifies the proverb that there is no honor among thieves
   B. is full of corruption, plots, and intrigue
   C. is principally concerned with the welfare of its own people
   D. would plot with other governments to advance their own mutual interests

Questions 16-17.

DIRECTIONS: Questions 16 and 17 are to be answered SOLELY on the basis of the following passage.

A gentleman is mainly occupied in removing the obstacles which hinder the free and unembarrassed action of those about him; and he concurs with their movements rather than takes the initiative himself. The true gentleman carefully avoids whatever may cause a jar or jolt in the minds of those with whom he is cast. His great concern is to put everyone at his ease and to make all feel at home. He is tender towards the bashful, gentle towards the distant, and merciful towards the absurd; he can recollect to whom he is speaking; he guards against unseasonable allusions, or topics which may irritate; he is seldom prominent in conversation, and never wearisome.

16. According to the above passage, a gentleman makes it his business to   16.____

    A.   discuss current issues of interest although controversial
    B.   get the bashful to participate in the conversation
    C.   introduce to one another guests who have not previously met
    D.   remember the person with whom he is speaking

17. According to the above passage, one of the CHIEF characteristics of a gentleman is that   17.____
he

    A.   conducts himself in such a way as to avoid hurting the feelings of others
    B.   keeps the conversation going, particularly when interest flags
    C.   puts an unruly guest in his place politely but firmly
    D.   shows his guests the ways in which they can best enjoy

18. Too often we retire people who are willing and able to continue working, according to   18.____
Federal Security Agency Administrator Oscar R. Ewing in addressing the first National
Conference on Aging; to point up the fact that chronological age is no longer an effective
criterion in determining whether or not an individual is capable of working. The Second
World War proved this point when it became necessary to hire older, experienced people
to handle positions in business and industry vacated by personnel called to serve their
country. As shown by production records set during the war period, the employment of
older people helped us continue, and even better, our high level of production.
It was also pointed out at the conference that our life expectancy is increasing and that
the over-65 group will jump from 11,500,000 now to twenty million in 2015. A good
many of these people are capable of producing and have a desire to work, but they are
kept from gainful employment by a shortsightedness on the part of many employers
which leads them to believe that young people alone can give them adequate service.
It is true that the young person has greater agility and speed to offer, but on the other
hand there is much to be gained from the experience, steadfastness, and maturity of
judgment of the elderly worker.
The title that BEST expresses the ideas of the above passage is

    A.   INCREASED EFFICIENCY OF ELDERLY WORKERS
    B.   MISJUDGING ELDERLY WORKERS
    C.   LENGTHENING THE SPAN OF LIFE
    D.   NEW JOBS FOR THE AGED

19. The question is whether night baseball will prove a boon or a disaster to the game. The   19.__
    big crowds now attending the night games, the brilliance of the spectacle, the miracle of
    the spinning turnstiles all these seem sufficient evidence that what is needed is not less
    night ball, but more. The fact remains, however, that despite all apparent success, some
    of the shrewdest, most experienced men in baseball remain unconvinced of the miracle.
    They are steady in their preference for daytime baseball, and they view with increasing
    distrust the race towards more lights. It could be that these men are simply being obsti-
    nate. Yet, on the other hand, it could be that in reviewing the caliber of baseball as it is
    played at night, in speculating upon the future effect of night ball, they are not entirely
    unprophetic. It could even be, indeed, that they are dead right.
    In his attitude toward the future of night baseball, the author expresses

    A. uncertainty   B. confidence
    C. optimism   D. sharp criticism

20. We all know people who would welcome a new American car to their stables, but one   20.__
    cannot expect to find a sports car man among them. He cannot be enticed into such a
    circus float without feeling soiled. He resents the wanton use of chromium as much as he
    shudders at the tail fins, the grotesquely convoluted bumpers, and other *dishonest* lines.
    He blanches at the enormous bustle that adds weight and useless space, drags on
    ramps and curbstones, and complicates the process of parking even in the car's own
    garage. The attitude of the owner of a Detroit product is reflected in the efforts of manu-
    facturers to *take the drive out of driving*. The sports car addict regards this stand as out-
    rageous. His interest in a car, he is forever telling himself and other captive listeners, lies
    in the fun of driving it, in *sensing its alertness on the road*, and in *pampering it as a thor-
    oughbred.*
    The above passage implies that sports cars are very

    A. colorful   B. showy
    C. maneuverable   D. roomy

Questions 21-25.

DIRECTIONS: Questions 21 through 25 are to be answered SOLELY on the basis of the fol-
              lowing passage.

Fuel is conserved when a boiler is operating near its most efficient load. The efficiency of
a boiler will change as the output varies. Large amounts of air must be used at low ratings
and so the heat exchanger is inefficient. As the output increases, the efficiency decreases
due to an increase in flue gas temperature. Every boiler has an output rate for which its efficiency is highest. For example, in a water-tube boiler, the highest efficiency might occur at
120 percent of rated capacity while in a vertical fire-tube boiler highest efficiency might be at
70% of rated capacity. The type of fuel burned and cleanliness affects the maximum efficiency of the boiler. When a power plant contains a battery of boilers, a sufficient number
should be kept in operation so as to maintain the output of individual units near their points of
maximum efficiency. One of the boilers in the battery can be used as a regulator to meet the
change in demand for steam while the other boilers could still operate at their most efficient
rating. Boiler performance is expressed as the number of pounds of steam generated per
pound of fuel.

21. According to the above paragraph, the number of pounds of steam generated per pound   21.____
of fuel is a measure of boiler

    A. size   B. performance
    C. regulator input   D. bypass

22. According to the above paragraph, the HIGHEST efficiency of a vertical fire tube boiler   22.____
might occur at _____ capacity.

    A. 70% of rate   B. 80% of water tube
    C. 95% of water tube   D. 120% of rated

23. According to the above paragraph, the MAXIMUM efficiency of a boiler is affected by   23.____

    A. atmospheric temperature   B. atmospheric pressure
    C. cleanliness   D. fire brick material

24. According to the above paragraph, a heat exchanger uses large amounts of air at low   24.____

    A. fuel rates   B. ratings
    C. temperatures   D. pressures

25. According to the above paragraph, one boiler in a battery of boilers should be used as a   25.____

    A. demand   B. stand-by
    C. regulator   D. safety

KEY (CORRECT ANSWERS)

1.	D		11.	D
2.	D		12.	A
3.	D		13.	C
4.	D		14.	D
5.	C		15.	D
6.	B		16.	D
7.	A		17.	A
8.	D		18.	B
9.	C		19.	A
10.	B		20.	C

21.	B
22.	A
23.	C
24.	B
25.	C

TEST 3

DIRECTIONS: Questions 1 through 7 are to be answered SOLELY on the basis of the follow-ing paragraph on FIRST AID INSTRUCTIONS.

FIRST AID INSTRUCTIONS

The main purpose of first aid is to put the injured person in the best possible position until medical help arrives. This includes the performance of emergency treatment designed to save a life if a doctor is not immediately available. When an accident happens, a crowd usu-ally collects around the victim. If nobody uses his head, the injured person fails to receive the care he needs. You must keep calm and cool at all times and, most important, it is your duty to take charge at an accident. The first thing for you to do is to see, insofar as possible, what is wrong with the injured person. Leave him where he is until the nature and extent of his injury are determined. If he is unconscious, he should not be moved except to lay him flat on his back if he is in some other position. Loosen the clothing of any seriously hurt person, and make him as comfortable as possible. Medical help should be called as soon as possible. You should remain with the injured person and send someone else to call the doctor. You should try to make sure that the one who calls for a doctor is able to give correct information as to the location of the injured person. In order to help the physician to know what equipment may be needed in each particular case, the person making the call should give the doctor as much information about the injury as possible.

1. If nobody uses his head at the scene of an accident, there is danger that   1.___

    A.   a large crowd will gather
    B.   emergency treatment will be needed
    C.   names of witnesses will be missed
    D.   the victim will not get the care he needs

2. The FIRST thing you should do at the scene of an accident is to   2.___

    A.   call a doctor
    B.   lay the injured person on his back
    C.   find out what is wrong with the injured person
    D.   loosen the clothing of the injured person

3. Until the nature and extent of the injuries are determined you should   3.___

    A.   move the injured person indoors
    B.   let the injured person lie where he is
    C.   carefully roll the injured person on his back
    D.   give the injured person artificial respiration

4. If the injured person is unconscious, you should   4.___

    A.   give him artificial respiration
    B.   get some hot liquid like coffee into him
    C.   lay him flat on his back
    D.   move him to a comfortable location

5. If a doctor is to be called, you should   5.____

    A. go make this call yourself since you have all the information
    B. go make this call yourself since you are in charge
    C. send someone who knows what happened
    D. send someone who is fast

6. The person calling the doctor should give as much information as he has regarding the   6.____
injury so that the doctor

    A. can bring the necessary equipment
    B. can decide whether he should come
    C. will know whom to notify
    D. can advise what should be done

7. The MAIN purpose of first aid is to   7.____

    A. stop bleeding
    B. prevent further complications of the injury
    C. keep the patient comfortable
    D. determine what the injuries are

Questions 8-13.

DIRECTIONS: Questions 8 through 13 are to be answered SOLELY on the basis of the following passage regarding selection of tours of duty.

SELECTION OF TOURS OF DUTY

A selection of tours of duty for the winter season for Railroad Porters will begin on Monday, December 27, and conclude on Thursday, December 30.

The selection will take place in Room 828, 8th Floor, 370 Jay Street, Telephone Elmer 2-
5000, Extension 3870.

Railroad Porters whose names appear on the attached schedule will make selections at
the time and date indicated.

8. The selection of tours of duty began on   8.____

    A. Monday   B. Tuesday
    C. Wednesday   D. Thursday

9. No selections of tours of duty were scheduled for December   9.____

    A. 28   B. 29
    C. 30   D. 31

10. The choice of tours of duty was PROBABLY based on   10.____

    A. age   B. seniority
    C. borough of residence   D. alphabetical listing of names

11. The season for which the selection of tours of duty was made was the   11.___

    A. spring   B. summer
    C. autumn   D. winter

12. A porter making a selection had to do so   12.___

    A. before work   B. after work
    C. on his day off   D. at the time indicated

13. The selecting was to be done by   13.___

    A. all station employees
    B. all porters
    C. only the porters whose names were on the schedule
    D. employees not satisfied with present schedules

Questions 14-16.

DIRECTIONS: Questions 14 through 16 are to be answered SOLELY on the basis of the following passage concerning car inspection and cleaning information.

RIGID INSPECTION: Subway cars are hauled into a repair yard and given a rigid inspection about three times a month.

SWEEPING AND WASHING: Each car is swept every twenty-four hours. Its Windows are washed every time it comes into a repair yard.

OVERHAUL: At the completion of 90,000 miles, the car is almost completely taken apart, cleaned, and painted.

14. Car windows are USUALLY washed at least once in   14._

    A. one day   B. three days
    C. ten days   D. three months

15. If the average car traveled about 75,000 miles per year, it would NORMALLY be almost   15._
completely taken apart, cleaned, and painted about every

    A. 9 months   B. year
    C. 15 months   D. 2 years

16. If a car has been overhauled at the end of 90,000 miles, it would be brought back to the   16.
repair yard

    A. within one week for sweeping
    B. within two weeks for another overhaul
    C. after 90,000 miles for inspection if necessary
    D. within two weeks for a rigid inspection

Questions 17-19.

DIRECTIONS: Questions 17 through 19 are to be answered SOLELY on the basis of the following passage.

Into the nine square miles that make up Manhattan's business districts, about two million people travel each weekday to go to work-the equivalent of the combined populations of Boston, Baltimore, and Cincinnati. Some 140,000 drive there in cars, 200,000 take buses, and 100,000 ride the commuter railroads. The great majority, however, go by subway approximately 1.4 million people.

It is some ride. The last major improvement in the subway system was completed in 1935. The subways are dirty and noisy. Many local lines operate well beneath capacity, but many express lines are strained way beyond capacity—in particular, the lines to Manhattan, now overloaded by 39,000 passengers during peak hours.

But for all its discomforts, the subway system is inherently a far more efficient way of moving people than automobiles and highways. Making this system faster, more convenient, and more comfortable for people must be the core of the City's transportation effort.

17.   The CENTRAL point of the above passage is that   17.____

   A.   the equivalent of the combined populations of Boston, Baltimore, and Cincinnati commute into Manhattan's business district each weekday
   B.   the improvement of the subway system is the key to the solution of moving people efficiently in and out of Manhattan's business district
   C.   the subways are dirty and noisy, resulting in a terrible ride
   D.   we should increase the ability of people to get in and out of Manhattan by cars, subways, and commuter railroads in order to ease the load from the subways.

18.   In accordance with the above passage, 1.4 million people commute by subway and   18.____
   _____ by other mass transportation means.

   A.   200,000   B.   100,000
   C.   440,000   D.   300,000

19.   From the information given in the above passage, one could logically conclude that, next   19.____
   to the subways, the transportation system that carries the LARGEST number of passengers is

   A.   railroads   B.   cars
   C.   buses   D.   local lines

Questions 20-25.

DIRECTIONS: Questions 20 through 25 are to be answered SOLELY on the basis of the following passage. Each question consists of a statement. You are to indicate whether the statement is TRUE (T) or FALSE (F).

THE CITY

The City, which at one time in 1789-90 was the capital of the nation and which was also the capital of the State until 1796, has continued as the financial and economic capital of the United States and has grown to be the greatest city in the country.

The City is great because it has such a large population-a total of eight million persons in 2008. This population is larger than the total inhabitants of 41 of 75 of the largest countries in the world. The City requires many homes and buildings to accommodate its residents. The City consists of more than 725,000 buildings, more than half of which are one and two family houses owned by the occupants. More than five hundred hotels, with 128,000 rooms, are needed to take care of the visitors to the City; it is estimated that between one and two hundred thousand people visit the City daily.

The harbor is so large that any six of the other leading seaports of the world could be placed in it. Its piers, to accommodate freight and passengers, number 471, and its waterfront covers 770 miles.

20. The City has been the capital of the United States and also the capital of the State.   20.__

21. In 1988, the population of the City was greater than the total population of forty-one of   21.__
seventy-five of the largest countries in the world.

22. Over half of all the buildings in the City are one and two family homes which are owned   22.__
by the people who live in them?

23. A little under 200,000 people visit the City each year.   23.__

24. The harbor is larger than any other leading seaport.   24.__

25. The harbor is 471 miles long and has 770 piers to take care of passengers and cargo.   25.__

———

KEY (CORRECT ANSWERS)

1.	D	11.	D
2.	C	12.	D
3.	B	13.	C
4.	C	14.	C
5.	C	15.	C
6.	A	16.	D
7.	B	17.	B
8.	A	18.	D
9.	D	19.	C
10.	B	20.	T

21.	T
22.	T
23.	F
24.	T
25.	F

———

READING COMPREHENSION
UNDERSTANDING AND INTERPRETING WRITTEN MATERIAL
EXAMINATION SECTION
TEST 1

DIRECTIONS: Each question or incomplete statement is followed by several suggested answers or completions. Select the one that BEST answers the question or completes the statement. *PRINT THE LETTER OF THE CORRECT ANSWER IN THE SPACE AT THE RIGHT.*

Questions 1-4.

DIRECTIONS: Questions 1 through 4 are to be answered SOLELY on the basis of the following paragraph.

An annual leave allowance, which combines leaves previously given for vacation, personal business, family illness, and other reasons shall be granted members. Calculation of credits for such leave shall be on an annual basis beginning January 1st of each year. Annual leave credits shall be based on time served by members during preceding calendar year. However, when credits have been accrued and member retires during current year, additional annual leave credits shall, in this instance, be granted at accrual rate of three days for each completed month of service, excluding terminal leave. If accruals granted for completed months of service extend into following month, member shall be granted an additional three days accrual for completed month. This shall be the only condition where accruals in a current year are granted for vacation period in such year.

1. According to the above paragraph, if a fireman's wife were to become seriously ill so that he would take time off from work to be with her, such time off would be deducted from his _____ allowance.

    A. annual leave   B. vacation leave
    C. personal business leave   D. family illness leave

1.____

2. Terminal leave means leave taken

    A. at the end of the calendar year
    B. at the end of the vacation year
    C. immediately before retirement
    D. before actually earned, because of an emergency

2.____

3. A fireman appointed on July 1, 2007 will be able to take his first full or normal annual leave during the period

    A. July 1, 2007 to June 30, 2008
    B. Jan. 1, 2008 to Dec. 31, 2008
    C. July 1, 2008 to June 30, 2009
    D. Jan. 1, 2009 to Dec. 31, 2009

3.____

4. According to the above paragraph, a member who retires on July 15 of this year will be entitled to receive leave allowance based on this year of _____ days.   4.____

   A. 15   B. 18   C. 22   D. 24

5. Fire alarm boxes are electromechanical devices for transmitting a coded signal. In each box, there is a trainwork of wheels. When the box is operated, a spring-activated code wheel within begins to revolve. The code number of the box is notched on the circumference of the code wheel, and the latter is associated with the circuit in such a way that when it revolves it causes the circuit to open and close in a predetermined manner, thereby transmitting its particular signal to the central station. A fire alarm box is nothing more than a device for interrupting the flow of current in a circuit in such a way as to produce a coded signal that may be decoded by the dispatchers in the central office. Based on the above, select the FALSE statement: 5.____

   A. Each standard fire alarm box has its own code wheel
   B. The code wheel operates when the box is pulled
   C. The code wheel is operated electrically
   D. Only the break in the circuit by the notched wheel causes the alarm signal to be transmitted to the central office

Questions 6-9.

DIRECTIONS: Questions 6 through 9 are to be answered SOLELY on the basis of the following paragraph.

Ventilation, as used in fire fighting operations, means opening up a building or structure in which a fire is burning to release the accumulated heat, smoke, and gases. Lack of knowledge of the principles of ventilation on the part of firemen may result in unnecessary punishment due to ventilation being neglected or improperly handled. While ventilation itself extinguishes no fires, when used in an intelligent manner, it allows firemen to get at the fire more quickly, easily, and with less danger and hardship.

6. According to the above paragraph, the MOST important result of failure to apply the principles of ventilation at a fire may be   6.__

   A. loss of public confidence
   B. waste of water
   C. excessive use of equipment
   D. injury to firemen

7. It may be inferred from the above paragraph that the CHIEF advantage of ventilation is that it   7._

   A. eliminates the need for gas masks
   B. reduces smoke damage
   C. permits firemen to work closer to the fire
   D. cools the fire

8. Knowledge of the principles of ventilation, as defined in the above paragraph, would be LEAST important in a fire in a   8.____

    A. tenement house
    C. ship's hold
    B. grocery store
    D. lumberyard

9. We may conclude from the above paragraph that for the well-trained and equipped fire-man, ventilation is   9.____

    A. a simple matter
    C. relatively unimportant
    B. rarely necessary
    D. a basic tool

Questions 10-13.

DIRECTIONS: Questions 10 through 13 are to be answered SOLELY on the basis of the following passage.

Fire exit drills should be established and held periodically to effectively train personnel to leave their working area promptly upon proper signal and to evacuate the building, speedily but without confusion. All fire exit drills should be carefully planned and carried out in a serious manner under rigid discipline so as to provide positive protection in the event of a real emergency. As a general rule, the local fire department should be furnished advance information regarding the exact date and time the exit drill is scheduled. When it is impossible to hold regular drills, written instructions should be distributed to all employees.

Depending upon individual circumstances, fires in warehouses vary from those of fast development that are almost instantly beyond any possibility of employee control to others of relatively slow development where a small readily attackable flame may be present for periods of time up to 15 minutes or more during which simple attack with fire extinguishers or small building hoses may prevent the fire development. In any case, it is characteristic of many warehouse fires that at a certain point in development they flash up to the top of the stack, increase heat quickly, and spread rapidly. There is a degree of inherent danger in attacking warehouse type fires, and all employees should be thoroughly trained in the use of the types of extinguishers or small hoses in the buildings and well instructed in the necessity of always staying between the fire and a direct pass to an exit.

10.   Employees should be instructed that, when fighting a fire, they MUST   10.____

    A. try to control the blaze
    B. extinguish any fire in 15 minutes
    C. remain between the fire and a direct passage to the exit
    D. keep the fire between themselves and the fire exit

11.   Whenever conditions are such that regular fire drills cannot be held, then which one of the following actions should be taken?   11.____

    A. The local fire department should be notified.
    B. Rigid discipline should be maintained during work hours.
    C. Personnel should be instructed to leave their working area by whatever means are available.
    D. Employees should receive fire drill procedures in writing.

12. The above passage indicates that the purpose of fire exit drills is to train employees to   12.____

    A. control a fire before it becomes uncontrollable
    B. act as firefighters
    C. leave the working area promptly
    D. be serious

13. According to the above passage, fire exit drills will prove to be of UTMOST effectiveness   13.____
if

    A. employee participation is made voluntary
    B. they take place periodically
    C. the fire department actively participates
    D. they are held without advance planning

Questions 14-16.

DIRECTIONS: Questions 14 through 16 are to be answered SOLELY on the basis of the following paragraph.

The heat output from unit heaters will depend on how fast and how completely dry hot steam fills the unit core. For complete and fast air removal and rapid drainage of condensate, use a trap actuated by water or vapor (inverted bucket trap) and not a trap operated by temperature only (thermostatic or bellows trap). A temperature-actuated trap will hold back the hot condensate until it cools to a point where the thermal element opens. When this happens, the condensate backs up in the heater and reduces the heat output. With a water-actuated trap, this will not happen as the water or condensate is discharged as fast as it is formed.

14. On the basis of the information given in the above paragraph, it can be concluded that   14.__
the PROPER type of trap to use for a unit heater is a(n) _____ trap.

    A. thermostatic   B. bellows-type
    C. inverted bucket   D. temperature

15. According to the above paragraph, the MAIN reason for using the type of trap specified   15.__
for a unit heater is to

    A. bring the condensate up to steam temperature
    B. prevent reduction in the heat output of the unit heater
    C. permit cycling of the heater
    D. maintain constant temperature of condensate in the trap

16. As used in the above paragraph, the word *actuated* means MOST NEARLY   16._

    A. clogged   B. operated   C. cleaned   D. vented

Question 17 -25.

DIRECTIONS: Questions 17 through 25 are to be answered SOLELY on the basis of the following passage. Each question consists of a statement. You are to indicate whether the statement is TRUE (T) or FALSE (F).

MOVING AN OFFICE

An office with all its equipment is sometimes moved during working hours. This is a difficult task and must be done in an orderly manner to avoid confusion. The operation should be planned in such a way as not to interrupt the progress of work usually done in the office and to make possible the accurate placement of the furniture and records in the new location. If the office moves to a place inside the same building, the desks and files are moved with all their contents. If the movement is to another building, the contents of each desk and file are placed in boxes. Each box is marked with a letter showing the particular section in the new quarters to which it is to be moved. Also marked on each box is the number of the desk or file on which the box is to be placed. Each piece of equipment must have a numbered tag. The number of each piece of equipment is put in soft chalk on the floor in the new office to show the proper location, and several floor plans are made to show where each piece of equipment goes. When the moving is done, someone is stationed at each of the several exits of the old office to see that each box or piece of equipment has its destination clearly marked on it. At the new office, someone stands at each of the several entrances with a copy of the floor plan and directs the placing of the furniture and equipment according to the floor plan. No one should interfere at this point with the arrangements shown on the plan. Improvements in arrangement can be considered and made at a later date.

17. It is a hard job to move an office from one place to another during working hours.   17._____

18. Confusion cannot be avoided if an office is moved during working hours.   18._____

19. The work usually done in an office must be stopped for the day when the office is moved during working hours.   19._____

20. If an office is moved from one floor to another in the same building, the contents of a desk are taken out and put into boxes for moving.   20._____

21. If boxes are used to hold material from desks when moving an office, the box is numbered the same as the desk on which it is to be put.   21._____

22. Letters are marked in soft chalk on the floor at the new quarters to show where the desks should go when moved.   22._____

23. When the moving begins, a person is put at each exit of the old office to check that each box and piece of equipment has clearly marked on it where it to go.   23._____

24. A person stationed at each entrance of the new quarters to direct the placing of the furniture and equipment has a copy of the floor plan of the new quarters.   24._____

25. If, while the furniture is being moved into the new office, a person helping at a doorway gets an idea of a better way to arrange the furniture, he should change the planned arrangement and make a record of the change.   25._____

KEY (CORRECT ANSWERS)

1. A	11. D
2. C	12. C
3. D	13. B
4. B	14. C
5. C	15. B
6. D	16. B
7. C	17. T
8. D	18. F
9. D	19. F
10. C	20. F

21. T
22. F
23. T
24. T
25. F

———

TEST 2

DIRECTIONS: Questions 1 through 4 are to be answered SOLELY on the basis of the follow-
                ing paragraph.

In all cases of homicide, members of the Police Department who investigate will make every effort to obtain statements from dying persons. Such statements are of the greatest importance to the District Attorney. In many cases, there may be a failure to solve the crime if they are not taken. The principal element to be considered in taking the declaration of a dying person is his mental attitude. In order to be admissible in evidence, the person must have no hope of recovery. The patient will be fully interrogated on that point before a statement is taken.

1.   In cases of homicide, according to the above paragraph, members of the police force will   1._____

    A.   try to change the mental attitude of the dying person
    B.   attempt to obtain a statement from the dying person
    C.   not give the information they obtain directly to the District Attorney
    D.   be careful not to injure the dying person unnecessarily

2.   The mental attitude of the person making the dying statement is of GREAT importance   2._____
     because it can determine, according to the above paragraph, whether the

    A.   victim should be interrogated in the presence of witnesses
    B.   victim will be willing to make a statement of any kind
    C.   statement will tell the District Attorney who committed the crime
    D.   the statement can be used as evidence

3.   District Attorneys find that statements of a dying person are important, according to the   3._____
     above paragraph, because

    A.   it may be that the victim will recover and then refuse to testify
    B.   they are important elements in determining the mental attitude of the victim
    C.   they present a point of view
    D.   it may be impossible to punish the criminal without such a statement

4.   A well-known gangster is found dying from a bullet wound. The patrolman first on the   4._____
     scene, in the presence of witnesses, tells the man that he is going to die and asks, *Who
     shot you?* The gangster says, *Jones shot me, but he hasn't killed me. I'll live to get him.*
     He then falls back dead. According to the above paragraph, this statement is

    A.   *admissible* in evidence; the man was obviously speaking the truth
    B.   *not admissible* in evidence; the man obviously did not believe that he was dying
    C.   *admissible* in evidence; there were witnesses to the statement
    D.   *not admissible* in evidence; the victim did not sign any statement and the evidence
        is merely hearsay

Questions 5-7.

DIRECTIONS: Questions 5 through 7 are to be answered SOLELY on the basis of the follow-
                ing paragraph.

The factors contributing to crime and delinquency are varied and complex. The home and its immediate environment have been found to be crucial in determining the behavior patterns of the individual, and criminality can frequently be traced to faulty family relationships and a bad neighborhood. But in the search for a clearer understanding of the underlying causes of delinquent and criminal behavior, the total environment must be taken into consideration.

5. According to the above paragraph, family relationships   5.____

    A. tend to become faulty in bad neighborhoods
    B. are important in determining the actions of honest people as well as criminals
    C. are the only important element in the understanding of causes of delinquency
    D. are determined by the total environment

6. According to the above paragraph, the causes of crime and delinquency are   6.____

    A. not simple   B. not meaningless
    C. meaningless   D. simple

7. According to the above paragraph, faulty family relationships FREQUENTLY are   7.__

    A. responsible for varied and complex results
    B. caused when one or both parents have a criminal behavior pattern
    C. independent of the total environment
    D. the cause of criminal acts

Questions 8-10.

DIRECTIONS: Questions 8 through 10 are to be answered SOLELY on the basis of the following paragraph.

A change in the specific problems which confront the police and in the methods for dealing with them has taken place in the last few decades. The automobile is a two-way symbol of this change in policing. It menaces every city with a complicated traffic problem and has speeded up the process of committing a crime and making a getaway, but at the same time has increased the effectiveness of police operations. However, the major concern of police departments continues to be the antisocial or criminal actions and behavior of human beings.

8. On the basis of the above paragraph, it can be stated that, for the most part, in the past few decades the specific problems of a police force   8._

    A. have changed but the general problems have not
    B. as well as the general problems have changed
    C. have remained the same but the general problems have changed
    D. as well as the general problems have remained the same

9. According to the above paragraph, advances in science and industry have, in general, made the police   9._

    A. operations less effective from the overall point of view
    B. operations more effective from the overall point of view
    C. abandon older methods of solving police problems
    D. concern themselves more with the antisocial acts of human beings

10. The automobile is a *two-way symbol,* according to the above paragraph, because its use   10.____

   A. has speeded up getting to and away from the scene of a crime
   B. both helps and hurts police operations
   C. introduces a new antisocial act–traffic violation–and does away with criminals like horse thieves
   D. both increases and decreases speed by introducing traffic problems

Questions 11-14.

DIRECTIONS: Questions 11 through 14 are to be answered SOLELY on the basis of the following passage on INSTRUCTIONS TO COIN AND TOKEN CASHIERS.

INSTRUCTIONS TO COIN AND TOKEN CASHIERS

Cashiers should reset the machine registers to an even starting number before commencing the day's work. Money bags received directly from collecting agents shall be counted and receipted for on the collecting agent's form. Each cashier shall be responsible for all coin or token bags accepted by him. He must examine all bags to be used for bank deposits for cuts and holes before placing them in use. Care must be exercised so that bags are not cut in opening them. Each bag must be opened separately and verified before another bag is opened. The machine register must be cleared before starting the count of another bag. The amount shown on the machine register must be compared with the amount on the bag tag. The empty bag must be kept on the table for re-examination should there be a difference between the amount on the bag tag and the amount on the machine register.

11. A cashier should BEGIN his day's assignment by   11.____

   A. counting and accepting all money bags
   B. resetting the counting machine register
   C. examining all bags for cuts and holes
   D. verifying the contents of all money bags

12. In verifying the amount of money in the bags received from the collecting agent, it is BEST to   12.____

   A. check the amount in one bag at a time
   B. base the total on the amount on the collecting agent's form
   C. repeat the total shown on the bag tag
   D. refer to the bank deposit receipt

13. A cashier is instructed to keep each empty coin bag on. his table while verifying its contents CHIEFLY because, long as the bag is on the table,   13.____

   A. it cannot be misplaced
   B. the supervisor can see how quickly the cashier works
   C. cuts and holes are easily noticed
   D. a recheck is possible in case the machine count disagrees with the bag tag total

14. The INSTRUCTIONS indicate that it is NOT proper procedure for a cashier to   14.____

    A. assume that coin bags are free of cuts and holes
    B. compare the machine register total with the total shown on the bag tag
    C. sign a form when he receives coin bags
    D. reset the machine register before starting the day's counting

Questions 15-17.

DIRECTIONS: Questions 15 through 17 are to be answered SOLELY on the basis of the fol-
               lowing passage.

The mass media are an integral part of the daily life of virtually every American. Among these media the youngest, television, is the most pervasive. Ninety-five percent of American homes have at least one T.V. set, and on the average that set is in use for about 40 hours each week. The central place of television in American life makes this medium the focal point of a growing national concern over the effects of media portrayals of violence on the values, attitudes, and behavior of an ever increasing audience.

In our concern about violence and its causes, it is easy to make television a scapegoat. But we emphasize the fact that there is no simple answer to the problem of violence — no sin-gle explanation of its causes, and no single prescription for its control. It should be remem-bered that America also experienced high levels of crime and violence in periods before the advent of television.

The problem of balance, taste, and artistic merit in entertaining programs on television are complex. We cannot <u>countenance</u> government censorship of television. Nor would we seek to impose arbitrary limitations on programming which might jeopardize television's abil-ity to deal in dramatic presentations with controversial social issues. Nonetheless, we are deeply troubled by television's constant portrayal of violence, not in any genuine attempt to focus artistic expression on the human condition, but rather in pandering to a public preoccu-pation with violence that television itself has helped to generate.

15. According to the above passage, television uses violence MAINLY   15.__

    A. to highlight the reality of everyday existence
    B. to satisfy the audience's hunger for destructive action
    C. to shape the values and attitudes of the public
    D. when it films documentaries concerning human conflict

16. Which one of the following statements is BEST supported by the above passage?   16.__

    A. Early American history reveals a crime pattern which is not related to television.
    B. Programs should give presentations of social issues and never portray violent acts.
    C. Television has proven that entertainment programs can easily make the balance
        between taste and artistic merit a simple matter.
    D. Values and behavior should be regulated by governmental censorship.

17. Of the following, which word has the same meaning as *countenance,* as used in the   17
    above passage?

    A. Approve   B. Exhibit   C. Oppose   D. Reject

DIRECTIONS: Questions 18 through 21 are to be answered SOLELY on the basis of the following passage.

Maintenance of leased or licensed areas on public parks or lands has always been a problem. A good rule to follow in the administration and maintenance of such areas is to limit the responsibility of any lessee or licensee to the maintenance of the structures and grounds essential to the efficient operation of the concession, not including areas for the general use of the public, such as picnic areas, public comfort stations, etc.; except where such facilities are leased to another public agency or where special conditions make such inclusion practicable, and where a good standard of maintenance can be assured and enforced. If local conditions and requirements are such that public use areas are included, adequate safeguards to the public should be written into contracts and enforced in their administration, to insure that maintenance by the concessionaire shall be equal to the maintenance standards for other park property.

18. According to the above passage, when an area on a public park is leased to a concessionaire, it is usually BEST to   18._____

   A. confine the responsibility of the concessionaire to operation of the facilities and leave the maintenance function to the park agency
   B. exclude areas of general public use from the maintenance obligation of the concessionaire
   C. make the concessionaire responsible for maintenance of the entire area including areas of general public use
   D. provide additional comfort station facilities for the area

19. According to the above passage, a valid reason for giving a concessionaire responsibility for maintenance of a picnic area within his leased area is that   19._____

   A. local conditions and requirements make it practicable
   B. more than half of the picnic area falls within his leased area
   C. the concessionaire has leased picnic facilities to another public agency
   D. the picnic area falls entirely within his leased area

20. According to the above passage, a precaution that should be taken when a concessionaire is made responsible for maintenance of an area of general public use in a park is   20._____

   A. making sure that another public agency has not previously been made responsible for this area
   B. providing the concessionaire with up-to-date equipment, if practicable
   C. requiring that the concessionaire take out adequate insurance for the protection of the public
   D. writing safeguards to the public into the contract

KEY (CORRECT ANSWERS)

1.	B		11.	B
2.	D		12.	A
3.	D		13.	D
4.	B		14.	A
5.	B		15.	B
6.	A		16.	A
7.	D		17.	A
8.	A		18.	B
9.	B		19.	A
10.	B		20.	D

———

TEST 3

Questions 1-5.

DIRECTIONS: Questions 1 through 5 are to be answered SOLELY on the basis of the following paragraph.

Physical inspections are an important tool for the examiner because he will have to decide the case in many instances on the basis of the inspection report. Most proceedings in a rent office are commenced by the filing of a written application or complaint by an interested party; that is, either the landlord or the tenant. Such an application or complaint must be filed in duplicate in order that the opposing party may be served with a copy of the application or complaint and thus be given an opportunity to answer and oppose it. Sometimes, a further opportunity is given the applicant to file a written rebuttal or reply to his adversary's answer. Often an examiner can make a determination or decision based on the written application, the answer, and the reply to the answer; and, of course, it would speed up operations if it were always possible to make decisions based on written documents only. Unfortunately, decisions can't always be made that way. There are numerous occasions where <u>disputed</u> issues of fact remain which cannot be <u>resolved</u> on the basis of the written statements of the parties. Typical examples are the following: The tenant claims that the refrigerator or stove or bathroom fixture is not functioning properly and the landlord denies this. It is obvious that in such cases an inspection of the accommodations is almost the only means of resolving such disputed issues.

1. According to the above paragraph,   1._____

    A. physical inspections are made in all cases
    B. physical inspections are seldom made
    C. it is sometimes possible to determine the facts in a case without a physical inspection
    D. physical inspections are made when it is necessary to verify the examiner's determination

2. According to the above paragraph, in MOST cases, proceedings are started by a(n)   2._____

    A. inspector discovering a violation
    B. oral complaint by a tenant or landlord
    C. request from another agency, such as the Building Department
    D. written complaint by a tenant or landlord

3. According to the above paragraph, when a tenant files an application with the rent office,   3._____
    the landlord is

    A. not told about the proceeding until after the examiner makes his determination
    B. given the duplicate copy of the application
    C. notified by means of an inspector visiting the premises
    D. not told about the proceeding until after the inspector has visited the Premises

4. As used in the above paragraph, the word *disputed* means MOST NEARLY   4._____

    A. unsettled   B. contested
    C. definite   D. difficult

5. As used in the above paragraph, the word *resolved* means MOST NEARLY   5._____

    A. settled   B. fixed   C. helped   D. amended

Questions 6-10.

DIRECTIONS: Questions 6 through 10 are to be answered SOLELY on the basis of the following paragraph.

    The examiner should order or request an inspection of the housing accommodations. His request for a physical inspection should be in writing, identify the accommodations and the landlord and the tenant, and specify <u>precisely</u> just what the inspector is to look for and report on. Unless this request is specific and lists <u>in detail</u> every item which the examiner wishes to be reported, the examiner will find that the inspection has not served its purpose and that even with the inspector's report, he is still in no position to decide the case due to loose ends which have not been completely tied up. The items that the examiner is interested in should be separately numbered on the inspection request and the same number referred to in the inspector's report. You can see what it would mean if an inspector came back with a report that did not cover everything. It may mean a tremendous waste of time and often require a re-inspection.

6. According to the above paragraph, the inspector makes an inspection on the order of   6._____

    A. the landlord
    B. the tenant
    C. the examiner
    D. both the landlord and the tenant

7. According to the above paragraph, the reason for numbering each item that an inspector reports on is so that   7._____

    A. the report is neat
    B. the report can be easily read and referred to
    C. none of the examiner's requests for information is missed
    D. the report will be specific

8. The one of the following items that is NOT necessarily included in the request for inspection is   8._____

    A. location of dwelling   B. name of landlord
    C. item to be checked   D. type of building

9. As used in the above paragraph, the word precisely means MOST NEARLY   9._____

    A. exactly   B. generally   C. Usually   D. strongly

10. As used in the above paragraph, the words in detail mean MOST NEARLY   10._____

    A. clearly   B. item by item
    C. substantially   D. completely

Questions 11-13.

DIRECTIONS: Questions 11 through 13 are to be answered SOLELY on the basis of the following passage.

The agreement under which a tenant rents property from a landlord is known as a lease.
Generally speaking, leases are classified as either short-term or long-term in duration. They
are further subdivided according to the method used to determine the amount of periodic rent
payments. Of the following types of lease in use, the more commonly used ones are the following:

1.   The straight or fixed lease is one in which rent may be paid in equal amounts
      throughout the duration of the lease. These are usually restricted to short-term leas-
      ing, or somewhat longer-term if clauses in the lease provide for periodic escalation of
      payments as the economy shifts.
2.   Percentage leasing, used for short-term commercial leasing, provides the landlord
      with a stipulated percentage of a tenant's gross sales from goods and services sold
      on the premises, in addition to a fixed amount of rent.
3.   The net lease, generally long-term (ten years or more), requires the tenant to pay all
      operating costs, including real estate taxes and insurance. In a net-net lease, the ten-
      ant further agrees to meet mortgage interest and principal payments.
4.   An escalated lease, which is a long-term lease, requires rent to be of a stipulated
      base amount which periodically is subject to escalation in accordance with cost-of-
      living index scales, or in direct proportion to taxes, insurance, and operating costs.

11.   Based on the information given in the passage, which type of lease is MOST likely to be   11._____
      advantageous to a landlord if there is a high rate of inflation? _____ lease.

      A.   Fixed   B.   Percentage   C.   Net   D.   Escalated

12.   On the basis of the above passage, which types of lease would generally be MOST suit-   12._____
      able for a well-established textile company which requires permanent facilities for its
      large operations?
      _____ lease and _____ lease.

      A.   Percentage; escalated   B.   Escalated; net
      C.   Straight; net   D.   Straight; percentage

13.   According to the above passage, the ONLY type of lease which assures the same   13._____
      amount of rent throughout a specified interval is the _____ lease.

      A.   straight   B.   percentage   C.   net-net   D.   escalated

Questions 14-15.

DIRECTIONS: Questions 14 and 15 are to be answered SOLELY on the basis of the following
passage.

If you like people, if you seek contact with them rather than hide yourself in a corner, if
you study your fellow men sympathetically, if you try consistently to contribute something to
their success and happiness, if you are reasonably generous with your thought and your time,
if you have a partial reserve with everyone but a seeming reserve with no one, you will get
along with your superiors, your subordinates, and the human race.

By the scores of thousands, precepts and platitudes have been written for the guidance of personal conduct. The odd part of it is that, despite all of this labor, most of the frictions in modern society arise from the individual's feeling of inferiority, his false pride, his vanity, his unwillingness to yield space to any other man and his consequent urge to throw his own weight around. Goethe said that the quality which best enables a man to renew his own life, in his relation to others, is his capability of renouncing particular things at the right moment in order warmly to embrace something new in the next.

14. On the basis of the above passage, it may be INFERRED that

    A. a person should be unwilling to renounce privileges
    B. a person should realize that loss of a desirable job assignment may come at an opportune moment
    C. it is advisable for a person to maintain a considerable amount of reserve in his relationship with unfamiliar people
    D. people should be ready to contribute generously to a worthy charity

15. Of the following, the MOST valid implication made by the above passage is that

    A. a wealthy person who spends a considerable amount of money entertaining his friends is not really getting along with them
    B. if a person studies his fellow men carefully and impartially, he will tend to have good relationships with them
    C. individuals who maintain seemingly little reserve in their relationships with people have in some measure overcome their own feelings of inferiority
    D. most precepts that have been written for the guidance of personal conduct in relationships with other people are invalid

Questions 16-17.

DIRECTIONS: Questions 16 and 17 are to be answered SOLELY on the basis of the following passage.

When a design for a new bank note of the Federal Government has been prepared by the Bureau of Engraving and Printing and has been approved by the Secretary of the Treasury, the engravers begin the work of cutting the design in steel. No one engraver does all the work. Each man is a specialist. One works only on portraits, another on lettering, another on scroll work, and so on. Each engraver, with a steel tool known as a graver, and aided by a powerful magnifying glass, carefully carves his portion of the design into the steel. He knows that one false cut or a slip of his tool, or one miscalculation of width or depth of line, may destroy the merit of his work. A single mistake means that months or weeks of labor will have been in vain. The Bureau is proud of the fact that no counterfeiter ever has duplicated the excellent work of its expert engravers.

16. According to the above passage, each engraver in the Bureau of Engraving and Printing

    A. must be approved by the Secretary of the Treasury before he can begin work on the design for a new bank note
    B. is responsible for engraving a complete design of a new bank note by himself
    C. designs new bank notes and submits them for approval to the Secretary of the Treasury
    D. performs only a specific part of the work of engraving a design for a new bank note

17.   According to the above passage,

    A.   an engraver's tools are not available to a counterfeiter
    B.   mistakes made in engraving a design can be corrected immediately with little delay in the work of the Bureau
    C.   the skilled work of the engravers has not been successfully reproduced by counterfeiter
    D.   careful carving and cutting by the engravers is essential to prevent damage to equipment

17.____

Questions 18-21.

DIRECTIONS: Questions 18 through 21 are to be answered SOLELY on the basis of the following passage.

In the late fifties, the average American housewife spent $4.50 per day for a family of four on food and 5.15 hours in food preparation, if all of her food was *home prepared;* she spent $5.80 per day and 3.25 hours if all of her food was purchased *partially prepared;* and $6.70 per day and 1.65 hours if all of her food was purchased *ready to serve.*

Americans spent about 20 billion dollars for food products in 1941. They spent nearly 70 billion dollars in 1958. They spent 25 percent of their cash income on food in 1958. For the same kinds and quantities of food that consumers bought in 1941, they would have spent only 16% of their cash income in 1958. It is obvious that our food does cost more. Many factors contribute to this increase besides the additional cost that might be attributed to processing. Consumption of more expensive food items, higher marketing margins, and more food eaten in restaurants are other factors.

The Census of Manufacturers gives some indication of the total bill for processing. The value added by manufacturing of food and kindred products amounted to 3.5 billion of the 20 billion dollars spent for food in 1941. In the year 1958, the comparable figure had climbed to 14 billion dollars.

18.   According to the above passage, the cash income of Americans in 1958 was MOST NEARLY _____ billion dollars.

    A.   11.2   B.   17.5   C.   70   D.   280

18.____

19.   According to the above passage, if Americans bought the same kinds and quantities of food in 1958 as they did in 1941, they would have spent MOST NEARLY _____ billion dollars.

    A.   20   B.   45   C.   74   D.   84

19.____

20.   According to the above passage, the percent increase in money spent for food in 1958 over 1941, as compared with the percentage increase in money spent for food processing in the same years,

    A.   was greater
    B.   was less
    C.   was the same
    D.   cannot be determined from the passage

20.____

21. In 1958, an American housewife who bought all of her food ready-to-serve saved in time,   21.____
as compared with the housewife who prepared all of her food at home

    A. 1.6 hours daily
    B. 1.9 hours daily
    C. 3.5 hours daily
    D. an amount of time which cannot be determined from the above passage

Questions 22-25.

DIRECTIONS: Questions 22 through 25 are to be answered SOLELY on the basis of the fol-
                lowing passage.

    Any member of the retirement system who is in city service, who files a proper applica-
tion for service credit and agrees to deductions from his compensation at triple his normal
rate of contribution, shall be credited with a period of city service previous to the beginning of
his present membership in the retirement system. The period of service credited shall be
equal to the period throughout which such triple deductions are made, but may not exceed
the total of the city service the member rendered between his first day of eligibility for membership in the retirement system and the day he last became a member. After triple contributions for all of the first three years of service credit claimed, the remaining service credit may
be purchased by a single payment of the sum of the remaining payments. If the total time pur-
chasable exceeds ten years, triple contributions may be made for one-half of such time, and
the remaining time purchased by a single payment of the sum of the remaining payments.
Credit for service acquired in the above manner may be used only in determining the amount
of any retirement benefit. Eligibility for such benefit will, in all cases, be based upon service
rendered after the employee's membership last began, and will be exclusive of service credit
purchased as described below.

22. According to the above passage, in order to obtain credit for city service previous to the   22.__
beginning of an employee's present membership in the retirement system, the employee
must

    A. apply for the service credit and consent to additional contributions to the retirement
       system
    B. apply for the service credit before he renews his membership in the retirement sys-
       tem
    C. have previous city service which does not exceed ten years
    D. make contributions to the retirement system for three years

23. According to the information in the above passage, credit for city service previous to the   23._
beginning of an employee's present membership in the retirement system, is

    A. credited up to a maximum of ten years
    B. credited to any member of the retirement system
    C. used in determining the amount of the employee's benefits
    D. used in establishing the employee's eligibility to receive benefits

24. According to the information in the above passage, a member of the retirement system may purchase service credit for

    A. the period of time between his first day of eligibility for membership in the retirement system and the date he applies for the service credit
    B. one-half of the total of his previous city service if the total time exceeds ten years
    C. the period of time throughout which triple deductions are made
    D. the period of city service between his first day of eligibility for membership in the retirement system and the day he last became a member

24.____

25. Suppose that a member of the retirement system has filed an application for service credit for five years of previous city service.
Based on the information in the above passage, the employee may purchase credit for this previous city service by making

    A. triple contributions for three years
    B. triple contributions for one-half of the time and a single payment of the sum of the remaining payments
    C. triple contributions for three years and a single payment of the sum of the remaining payments
    D. a single payment of the sum of the payments

25.____

KEY (CORRECT ANSWERS)

1. C	11. D		
2. D	12. B		
3. B	13. A		
4. B	14. B		
5. A	15. C		
6. C	16. D		
7. C	17. C		
8. D	18. D		
9. A	19. B		
10. B	20. B		

21. C
22. A
23. C
24. D
25. C
